TWELFTH NIGHT

The RSC Shakespeare

Edited by Jonathan Bate and Eric Rasmussen

Chief Associate Editors: Héloïse Sénéchal and Jan Sewell

Associate Editors: Trey Jansen, Eleanor Lowe, Lucy Munro,
Dee Anna Phares

Twelfth Night

Textual editing: Eric Rasmussen

Introduction and Shakespeare's Career in the Theater: Jonathan Bate

Commentary: Eleanor Lowe and Héloïse Sénéchal

Scene-by-Scene Analysis: Esme Miskimmin

In Performance: Karin Brown (RSC stagings), Jan Sewell (overview)

The Director's Cut (interviews by Jonathan Bate and Kevin Wright):
Sam Mendes, Declan Donnellan, and Neil Bartlett

The RSC Shakespeare

William Shakespeare

TWELFTH NIGHT

Edited by Jonathan Bate and Eric Rasmussen

Introduction by Jonathan Bate

The Modern Library
New York

CONTENTS

INTRODUCTION

"HOW HAVE YOU MADE DIVISION OF YOURSELF?"

"What is love?" asks Feste the clown in one of his songs. It is a very old question. One of the most influential answers to it comes from ancient Greece in the imaginary voice of the comic dramatist Aristophanes in Plato's dialogue called the *Symposium*. Love, says Aristophanes, is a quest, a journey in search of our lost other half.

The idea is explained by way of a story about human origins. Originally there were not two sexes but three—male, female, and a mixture of the two called androgynous. Furthermore, the original humans were round, with four hands, four feet, and two faces. Humankind then began to have presumptuous ambitions. We rose up against the Olympian gods. Zeus therefore decided to weaken us by cutting us in two, "like an apple halved for pickling." So now we have two legs, two arms, one face, and the sensation that we are only half ourselves. We yearn and wander, hoping that one day we will find the other half that is literally our soul mate. If the original whole of which you are a half was male, your desire will be for another male (as seems to be the case with Antonio in this play—and Orsino when he falls for "Cesario"?); if female, another female (Olivia desiring the disguised Viola?). These two orientations are what we now call homosexual.

Only if your original was androgynous will you be drawn to the opposite sex, as Viola is to Orsino—and Sir Toby, who has the play's largest role, to Maria. When one of us meets his or her other half, "the actual half of himself," then, the *Symposium* explains, "the pair are lost in an amazement of love and friendship and intimacy, and one will not wish to be out of the other's sight even for a moment: these are the people who pass their whole lives together, and yet they could not explain what they desire of one another."

A myth of this kind is a piece of storytelling that answers to a profound and enduring human belief: that we are somehow incomplete without love, without a partner. And that in an ideal world we would all have exactly the right partner. We know viscerally that desire and reproduction are forever bound to conjunction and splitting: two people join as one in the act of love; we are made out of a mixture of X and Y chromosomes, of male seed and female egg, of two distinct genetic lines.

If love is a quest for an idealized version of our own selves, it is easy to understand our fascination with twins. They seem to be the living embodiment of the single self split in two; the extreme case of conjoined twins vividly conjures up the *Symposium*'s tale of the original human as an unhalved apple. At the same time, a certain anxiety has always been attached to the phenomenon of twins. In ancient Greece it was assumed that a woman who bore twins must have been impregnated by two different men. Some mythical twins represent idealized unity—as with Castor and Pollux, the "gemini" or heavenly twins who symbolize perfect friendship—but others represent opposition or splitting. A nymph in Ovid's *Metamorphoses* has twins fathered by Apollo, god of music and light, and Mercury, god of theft and shady dealings; a pair of girl twins in Edmund Spenser's epic romance of Shakespeare's time, *The Faerie Queene*, respectively embody chastity and eroticism; in another of Ovid's poems, the *Fasti*, a girl called Lara is raped by Mercury and bears the Lares Compitales, who become guardians of the crossroads. These twins become symbolic of how the story of our lives is made of a perpetual sequence of choices, as alternative ways open before us.

Perhaps the most potent of all narratives about twins are those in which a brother and sister are separated soon after birth, meet when they are grown up and fall passionately and unashamedly in love with each other: Siegmund and Sieglinde, as portrayed in Richard Wagner's *Die Walküre*, might be considered Western culture's highest exemplar of the motif. Brother–sister incest was sometimes explored in the Renaissance theater—most notably in John Ford's darkly brilliant *'Tis Pity She's a Whore*—but Shakespeare steered away from this dangerous matter. His way of recreating the *Symposium*'s originary androgyne was by cross-dressing Viola as "Cesario," the lovely boy actor with whom both man and woman, both Orsino and Olivia, fall in love. Puns on "woman's part" and "small pipe" (meaning both

voice and male sexual organ) leave no doubt that alluring androg-
yny is implied here:

> For they shall yet belie thy happy years,
> That say thou art a man: Diana's lip
> Is not more smooth and rubious, thy small pipe
> Is as the maiden's organ, shrill and sound,
> And all is semblative a woman's part.

William and Ann Shakespeare's twins, Judith and Hamnet (alter-
natively spelled Hamlet), were born in February 1585. Their father's
fascination with the dramatic possibilities of double selves is apparent
from his early *Comedy of Errors*, where he adapted a classical story
about separated male twins and mistaken identity, but complicated it
by giving the brothers servants who are also identical twins. Then in
the summer of 1596, the eleven-year-old Hamnet died. Shakespeare
had lost his only son and Judith would be forever bereft of her second
self. Though we should always be wary of inferring authorial autobi-
ography from the words of fictional characters in a play, there is an
inescapable poignancy to the images of loss in *Twelfth Night*: when
Feste sings of sad cypress ("Come away, death") or Viola alludes to a
funeral monument, it is tempting to think of Shakespeare's own lost
boy. Olivia mourns a brother, while Viola assumes that hers has been
drowned. When she takes a male disguise and "becomes" Cesario, it
is as if she impersonates her own opposite-sex twin: "I am all the
daughters of my father's house, / And all the brothers too." She herself explains that the lost Sebastian is the model for her performance
of male behavior ("For him I imitate").

The principal source of *Twelfth Night*'s tale of siblings lost and
found, and of a cross-dressed servant sent to woo on behalf of a master whom she loves herself, was a novella by Barnaby Riche called
"Apollonius and Silla." There the brother and sister who are the origi-
nals for Viola and Sebastian are not twins but "the one of them was so
like the other in countenance and favour that there was no man able to
discern the one from the other by their faces, saving by their apparel,
the one being a man, the other a woman." Critics sometimes express
puzzlement that Shakespeare makes so much of the resemblance

between Viola and Sebastian, given his presumed personal knowledge that boy-girl twins are not identical. In modern terminology, it is generally accepted that monozygotic fertilization is always same sex (in fact, recent research has shown that in certain rare cases of genetic abnormality it is possible to have boy-girl monozygotic twins). But Riche's original premise reveals the absurdity of this criticism of the plot: siblings don't even have to be twins to look remarkably alike.

One of the greatest challenges for a writer is to imagine what it would be like to be a member of the opposite sex. The particular demand faced by Shakespeare and the boy actors who played his women's parts was to get beyond the age's conventions of proper female behavior, which commended silence and submissiveness. "Cesario" is partly a device to give Viola an active voice, to enable her to break the shackles of passivity. But the lovely combination of quick-witted facility, wonder, and vulnerability with which she slots into her impersonation is something more than a reaction to social convention or codes of propriety. In terms of the play's imaginary world, Viola plays Cesario so effectively because of her prior knowledge and love of Sebastian—this is what allows the otherwise implausible conceit of Olivia's marrying Sebastian in the belief that he is Cesario. In terms of the play's creative origin, it is tempting to speculate that the germ was sown by Shakespeare's observation of the intuitive understanding between his twins as they learned to speak and to play together.

Shakespearean comedy often imagines a journey from the secure womb of the family to a world of shipwreck and isolation, and thence to the bond of marriage. The characters lose themselves to find themselves. Broken families are restored in the same instant that new families are anticipated through the pronouncement of love vows. The climax of *Twelfth Night* is one of the great reunion scenes, as the parted twins are joined:

ORSINO   One face, one voice, one habit, and two persons,
    A natural perspective, that is and is not!
  . . .

ANTONIO   How have you made division of yourself?
    An apple cleft in two is not more twin
    Than these two creatures. . . .

The language is richly suggestive of one made two and two made one, of the cleft apple from the *Symposium*'s myth of origins, and of the workings of nature combined with the trick of art (a "perspective" was a distorting glass that created the optical illusion of one picture appearing as two). In a single action, brother and sister find both each other and their object of desire.

And yet. The peculiar poignancy of *Twelfth Night* comes from the sense that there are many losses even in this moment of wonder. Antonio, who has been like a brother and even a lover to Sebastian, is left alone. Malvolio has been humiliated just a little too far. The union of Sir Toby and Maria leaves Sir Andrew isolated—he was adored once, too, but we cannot imagine that he will be again. And Feste is there to sing another sad song of time and change. Above all, Cesario is no more: Orsino closes the dialogue by addressing Viola by her boy-name one final time before she assumes her female garb and becomes his "fancy's queen." But "fancy's queen" is the very language of that shallow courtly love with which Orsino had tried to woo Olivia: the language that Cesario cast off when he/she began speaking in his/her own voice. In the closing moments of the play, Viola does seem to revert to the silence and passivity of orthodox female behavior.

What is going through her imaginary heart at this moment? Even as Sebastian and Orsino are found, Cesario is lost. Could Viola be saying goodbye to the feigned twin into which she has made herself?

The name "Cesario" suggests untimely birth—as in "Cesarean section," a baby "from his mother's womb untimely ripped"—but the character undergoes an untimely death. A few months before starting the comedy of *Twelfth Night*, Shakespeare completed his deeply meditated tragedy of *Hamlet*. There are unfathomable crosscurrents at work here: in creating and destroying Cesario, perhaps Shakespeare too is saying a goodbye. To his own Hamnet. Viola is diminished when bereaved of her invented second self. Was this Shakespeare's delayed response to poor Judith's desolation on the loss of her twin?

In preparing to direct the play for the Royal Shakespeare Company in 2009, Gregory Doran, himself a twin, noticed a coincidence neglected by nearly all the legion of Shakespeare's biographers and critics. Hamnet and Judith Shakespeare were baptized on 2 February, the feast of Candlemas (which celebrates the presentation of the baby Jesus in the Temple in Jerusalem—a fitting moment for the baptism of a treasured first son). And it was on that very same festival day seventeen years later, 2 February, Candlemas, that *Twelfth Night* was performed (the earliest performance of which we have a record) before the law students of the Middle Temple in 1602. Malvolio describes Cesario/Viola as "Not yet old enough for a man, nor young enough for a boy. As a squash is before 'tis a peascod, or a codling when 'tis almost an apple: 'tis with him in standing water, between boy and man." On 2 February 1602, Judith was in standing water between girl and woman. By turning Viola into Cesario and allowing Sebastian to return from the devouring sea of death, Shakespeare allowed himself the consoling fantasy of a seventeenth birthday reunion for his own separated twins.

THE FOUNTAIN OF SELF-LOVE

A more immediate occasion for the play's meditations on love and identity seems to have been Shakespeare's friendly rivalry with Ben Jonson. Shakespeare had been writing courtship comedies for many years when Jonson came onto the theatrical scene at the end of the 1590s with a more hard-edged satirical vein of drama that tapped into the psychology of "humours"—the idea that aberrant behavior (which is readily comic and worthy of satire) could be attributed to an excess of a particular passion or obsession or to temperamental imbalance (too much choler or melancholy). Jonson seems to have fallen out with Shakespeare's acting company early in the new century. At this time he wrote a play called *The Fountain of Self-Love, or Cynthia's Revels* for the Children of Her Majesty's Chapel, the "boy-actors" company that, to judge from a famous piece of dialogue in *Hamlet*, was perceived by Shakespeare and his fellows as something of a threat to their own prestige. Jonson's double title was innovative and not a little pretentious: Shakespeare may well have been mocking it with *Twelfth Night, or What You Will* (his only double title). In pricking the bubble of inflated language, as he habitually does, Feste may be glancing at Jonson's verbosity. "I might say 'element,' but the word is over-worn": "element" is a key word in Jonson's humoral lexicon. And again, in response to Antonio's "I prithee vent thy folly somewhere else," Feste says "Vent my folly! He has heard that word of some great man and now applies it to a fool. Vent my folly!" Since *The Fountain of Self-Love* contains such phrases as "vent thy passion" and "vent the Etna of his fires," "some great man" might almost be Jonson.

The fountain in Jonson's play is that of Narcissus, who drowned while trying to kiss his own reflection. Shakespeare's Illyria is also a place of self-love. Yellow-stockinged Malvolio in particular is a Narcissus figure, but there is also a certain vanity about Orsino as he plays the role of the courtly lover. Viola, by contrast, is the opposite of a self-lover. She comes back from drowning and speaks in the voice of the desiring woman whom Narcissus neglected:

Make me a willow cabin at your gate,
And call upon my soul within the house,
Write loyal cantons of contemnèd love
And sing them loud even in the dead of night,
Hallow your name to the reverberate hills
And make the babbling gossip of the air
Cry out "Olivia!" O, you should not rest
Between the elements of air and earth,
But you should pity me!

As intimated by the "reverberate hills" and the echo effect "'Olivia!' O," the "babbling gossip of the air" alludes to the mythological figure of Echo, who pined away as a result of her unrequited love for Narcissus.

Jonsonian comedy is peopled by narcissists. *Twelfth Night* responds with an astonishing exploration of the relationship between knowledge of self and sympathy for others—which we might call "echoing"—in the composition of human identity. "I am not what I am"; "Be that thou know'st thou art"; "I swear I am not that I play"; "Ourselves we do not owe"; "Nothing that is so is so"; "You shall from this time be / Your master's mistress." These paradoxes and promises are the word-music of Illyria that "gives a very echo to the seat / Where love is throned."

MASTER-MISTRESS

The play begins with what sounds very like a fifteen-line unrhymed sonnet, spoken in the voice of an archetypal Renaissance lover, an aficionado of the great Italian poet Petrarch's sonnets in praise of his lovely but unobtainable Laura. This kind of love thrives on unrequitedness. The poet-lover uses imagery of music and the sea, of food, of rising and falling. Such language is typical of the vogue for sonneteering in the 1590s: every self-respecting Elizabethan poet had a sheaf of sonnets to his or her name. Like the conventional sonneteers, Orsino alludes to figures from classical mythology, in his case Ovid's Actaeon hunted down by the dogs of his own desire for lovely but chaste Diana. When Olivia appears, Orsino says that "heaven walks on earth," which is just what an orthodox sonneteer would say. He revels in the "sovereign cruelty" of his stony lady, as all Petrarchan lovers do.

But he is then thrown by the beauty of a lovely boy. The audience, however, knows that Cesario is really Viola, a girl in disguise, and that the body parts so lovingly blazoned by Orsino really are the "woman's part"—except they are not, since (at least the majority of) the audience also knows that Viola is a part written for a boy actor. "Thou dost speak masterly" says Orsino in response to Cesario's eloquence. In so doing, he allows himself to become the master mastered by the servingman. Or rather the boy. Or is that the girl? Or the boy actor?

Orsino claims that a woman's love is of less value than a man's because it is driven solely by "appetite," which may be sated, whereas his capacity for desire is infinite:

> There is no woman's sides
> Can bide the beating of so strong a passion
> As love doth give my heart, no woman's heart
> So big, to hold so much. They lack retention.
> Alas, their love may be called appetite,
> No motion of the liver, but the palate,
> That suffer surfeit, cloyment and revolt.
> But mine is all as hungry as the sea,
> And can digest as much. . . .

Here he again resembles a sonneteer, whose love is limitless because it is defined by being unrequited. And when he reappears at the end of the play, Orsino duly speaks another of his fifteen-line sonnets, this one ending with the most hackneyed rhyme in the sonneteer's repertoire:

> Why should I not, had I the heart to do it,
> Like to th'Egyptian thief at point of death,
> Kill what I love? — a savage jealousy
> That sometimes savours nobly. But hear me this:
> Since you to non-regardance cast my faith,
> And that I partly know the instrument
> That screws me from my true place in your favour,
> Live you the marble-breasted tyrant still.
> But this your minion, whom I know you love,
> And whom, by heaven I swear, I tender dearly,
> Him will I tear out of that cruel eye,
> Where he sits crownèd in his master's spite.
> Come, boy, with me. My thoughts are ripe in mischief:
> I'll sacrifice the lamb that I do love,
> To spite a raven's heart within a dove.

But then he discovers that Cesario is really Viola and he is able to resolve the tension—which is also the tension of Shakespeare's sonnets—between love for a lovely boy and desire for a woman:

> Your master quits you. And for your service done him,
> So much against the mettle of your sex,
> So far beneath your soft and tender breeding,
> And since you called me master for so long,
> Here is my hand. You shall from this time be
> Your master's mistress.

If Orsino is the conventional Elizabethan sonneteer, Olivia is parodist of the genre. The sonneteer customarily enumerates his lady's beautiful body parts, one by one in that device known as the "blazon." Olivia enumerates her own: "I will give out divers schedules of my beauty. It shall be inventoried, and every particle and utensil labelled to my will: as, *item*, two lips, indifferent red: *item*, two grey eyes, with lids to them: *item*, one neck, one chin and so forth." But then love—for Cesario—catches up on her and she finds herself deploying the blazon in all seriousness: "Thy tongue, thy face, thy limbs, actions and spirit, / Do give thee five-fold blazon." She begins to wish that "the master were the man"—or the man her master. Viola, meanwhile, gains a voice by becoming Cesario. In the sonnet form, the object of desire is just that, an object. In *Twelfth Night*, Viola, desired by both man and woman, is a feeling subject. Vulnerable, and thus forced to become an actor ("I am not that I play"), she soon finds herself in the situation of desiring the man she has been sent to persuade to love someone else—an analogous twist to that of Shakespeare's sonnets, which begin with the speaker persuading the fair youth to marry, then dissolve into the speaker's own love for the youth.

Sonnet 20 startlingly begins "A woman's face with Nature's own hand painted / Hast thou, the master-mistress of my passion." There is only one other phrase in the literature of the age that may be readily compared with the coinage "master-mistress": Orsino's "Your master's mistress." Perhaps as good an answer as any to the hoary old question of the identity of the lovely youth to whom the bulk of Shakespeare's sonnets are addressed is "a figure who resembles Cesario."

Twelfth Night is an extraordinary exploration of the permutations of desire or, to use the terminology of an Elizabethan admirer of Shakespeare called Francis Meres, of "the perplexities of love." Both Orsino and Olivia love Viola in her disguise as Cesario. Viola loves, and wins, Orsino, while Olivia has to settle for Sebastian. Orsino insists on continuing to call Viola Cesario even after he knows that she is a woman. Sebastian is puzzled, though grateful, to find himself whisked to the altar by the wealthy and beautiful Olivia, but he cannot have had time to fall in love with her. The person who really loves him is Antonio, who reminds him that for three months, "No interim, not a minute's vacancy, / Both day and night did we keep company." He follows his beloved despite the risk to his own life: "But come what may, I do adore thee so, / That danger shall seem sport, and I will go." Like a sonneteer, he speaks of being spurred on by his "desire, / More sharp than filèd steel" and, again, of paying "devotion" to "his image, which methought did promise / Most venerable worth." He is rewarded for his devotion by being left alone and melancholy, again in the exact manner of a sonneteer turned away by his frosty mistress. It is very easy to imagine Antonio going away at the end of *Twelfth Night* and writing something on the following lines, addressed to Sebastian:

> They that have power to hurt and will do none,
> That do not do the thing they most do show,
> Who, moving others, are themselves as stone,
> Unmovèd, cold, and to temptation slow:
> They rightly do inherit heaven's graces
> And husband nature's riches from expense.
> They are the lords and owners of their faces,
> Others but stewards of their excellence.

This is actually the speaker of Shakespeare's sonnets (in Sonnet 94) as he finds himself rejected by the fair youth or the lovely boy. In so many of the plays it is Shakespeare's chilly, self-controlled young men—Prince Hal in *Henry IV*, Angelo in *Measure for Measure*, Bertram in *All's Well That Ends Well*—who take, who are the lords and owners of their faces. His open hearted women—Rosalind in *As You Like It*, Innogen in *Cymbeline*, Viola above all—are never like this. They *do* do the things they most do show. They move others but they are never stone themselves, unless men turn them to coldness. His women give—of their selves, their wit, and their courage. And that is why his women's parts, even though written for boys, have been great gifts to actresses down the ages.

ABOUT THE TEXT

Shakespeare endures through history. He illuminates later times as well as his own. He helps us to understand the human condition. But he cannot do this without a good text of the plays. Without editions there would be no Shakespeare. That is why every twenty years or so throughout the last three centuries there has been a major new edition of his complete works. One aspect of editing is the process of keeping the texts up to date—modernizing the spelling, punctuation, and typography (though not, of course, the actual words), providing explanatory notes in the light of changing educational practices (a generation ago, most of Shakespeare's classical and biblical allusions could be assumed to be generally understood, but now they can't).

Because Shakespeare did not personally oversee the publication of his plays, with some plays there are major editorial difficulties. Decisions have to be made as to the relative authority of the early printed editions, the pocket format "quartos" published in Shakespeare's lifetime, and the elaborately produced "First Folio" text of 1623, the original "Complete Works" prepared for the press after his death by Shakespeare's fellow actors, the people who knew the plays better than anyone else. *Twelfth Night*, however, exists only in a Folio text that is exceptionally well printed. It is one of the few Shakespeare plays where there is hardly any textual difficulty or controversy.

The following notes highlight various aspects of the editorial process and indicate conventions used in the text of this edition:

Lists of Parts are supplied in the First Folio for only six plays, not including *Twelfth Night*, so the list here is editorially supplied. Capitals indicate that part of the name which is used for speech headings in the script (thus "SIR TOBY Belch, Olivia's kinsman").

Locations are provided by the Folio for only two plays, of which *Twelfth Night* is not one. Eighteenth-century editors, working in an age of elaborately realistic stage sets, were the first to provide detailed locations ("**another part of the town**"). Given that Shakespeare wrote for a bare stage and often an imprecise sense of place, we have relegated locations to the explanatory notes at the foot of the page, where they are given at the beginning of each scene where the imaginary location is different from the one before. In the case of *Twelfth Night*, the entire action is set in Illyria, on the eastern Adriatic coast, and moves principally between the households of Duke Orsino and Countess Olivia.

Act and Scene Divisions were provided in the Folio in a much more thoroughgoing way than in the Quartos. Sometimes, however, they were erroneous or omitted; corrections and additions supplied by editorial tradition are indicated by square brackets. Five-act division is based on a classical model, and act breaks provided the opportunity to replace the candles in the indoor Blackfriars playhouse which the King's Men used after 1608, but Shakespeare did not necessarily think in terms of a five-part structure of dramatic composition. The Folio convention is that a scene ends when the stage is empty. Nowadays, partly under the influence of film, we tend to consider a scene to be a dramatic unit that ends with either a change of imaginary location or a significant passage of time within the narrative. Shakespeare's fluidity of composition accords well with this convention, so in addition to act and scene numbers we provide a *running scene* count in the right margin at the beginning of each new scene, in the typeface used for editorial directions. Where there is a scene break caused by a momentary bare stage, but the location does not change and extra time does not pass, we use the convention *running scene continues*. There is inevitably a degree of editorial judgment in making such calls, but the system is very valuable in suggesting the pace of the plays.

Speakers' Names are often inconsistent in Folio. We have regularized speech headings, but retained an element of deliberate inconsistency in entry directions, in order to give the flavor of Folio. Thus FESTE is always so-called in his speech headings, but is generally "*Clown*" in entry directions.

Verse is indicated by lines that do not run to the right margin and by capitalization of each line. The Folio printers sometimes set verse as prose, and vice versa (either out of misunderstanding or for reasons of space). We have silently corrected in such cases, although in some instances there is ambiguity, in which case we have leaned toward the preservation of Folio layout. Folio sometimes uses contraction ("turnd" rather than "turned") to indicate whether or not the final "-ed" of a past participle is sounded, an area where there is variation for the sake of the five-beat iambic pentameter rhythm. We use the convention of a grave accent to indicate sounding (thus "turnèd" would be two syllables), but would urge actors not to overstress. In cases where one speaker ends with a verse half line and the next begins with the other half of the pentameter, editors since the late eighteenth century have indented the second line. We have abandoned this convention, since the Folio does not use it, nor did actors' cues in the Shakespearean theater. An exception is made when the second speaker actively interrupts or completes the first speaker's sentence.

Spelling is modernized, but older forms are very occasionally maintained where necessary for rhythm or aural effect.

Punctuation in Shakespeare's time was as much rhetorical as grammatical. "Colon" was originally a term for a unit of thought in an argument. The semicolon was a new unit of punctuation (some of the Quartos lack them altogether). We have modernized punctuation throughout, but have given more weight to Folio punctuation than many editors, since, though not Shakespearean, it reflects the usage of his period. In particular, we have used the colon far more than many editors: it is exceptionally useful as a way of indicating how many Shakespearean speeches unfold clause by clause in a developing argument that gives the illusion of enacting the process of thinking in the moment. We have also kept in mind the origin of punctuation in classical times as a way of assisting the actor and orator: the comma suggests the briefest of pauses for breath, the colon a middling one, and a full stop or period a longer pause. Semicolons, by contrast, belong to an era of punctuation that was only just coming in during Shakespeare's time and that is coming to an end now: we have accordingly only used them where they occur in our copy texts (and not always then). Dashes are sometimes used for parenthetical interjections where the Folio has brackets. They are also used for interruptions and changes in train of thought. Where a change of addressee occurs within a speech, we have used a dash preceded by a period (or occasionally another form of punctuation). Often the identity of the respective addressees is obvious from the context. When it is not, this has been indicated in a marginal stage direction.

Entrances and Exits are fairly thorough in Folio, which has accordingly been followed as faithfully as possible. Where characters are omitted or corrections are necessary, this is indicated by square brackets (e.g. "[*and Attendants*]"). *Exit* is sometimes silently normalized to *Exeunt* and *Manet* anglicized to "remains." We trust Folio positioning of entrances and exits to a greater degree than most editors.

Editorial Stage Directions such as stage business, asides, indications of addressee and of characters' position on the gallery stage are only used sparingly in Folio. Other editions mingle directions of this kind with original Folio and Quarto directions, sometimes marking them by means of square brackets. We have sought to distinguish what could be described as *directorial* interventions of this kind from Folio-style directions (either original or supplied) by placing them in the right margin in a different typeface. There is a degree of subjectivity about which directions are of which kind, but the procedure is intended as a reminder to the reader and the actor that Shakespearean stage directions are often dependent upon editorial inference alone and are not set in stone. We also depart from editorial tradition in sometimes admitting uncertainty and thus printing permissive stage directions, such as an **Aside?** (often a line may be equally effective as an aside or as a direct address—it is for each production or reading to make its own decision) or a ***may exit*** or a piece of business placed between arrows to indicate that it may occur at various different moments within a scene.

Line Numbers in the left margin are editorial, for reference and to key the explanatory and textual notes.

Explanatory Notes at the foot of each page explain allusions and gloss obsolete and difficult words, confusing phraseology, occasional major textual cruces, and so on. Particular attention is given to non-standard usage, bawdy innuendo, and technical terms (e.g. legal and military language). Where more than one sense is given, commas indicate shades of related meaning, slashes alternative or double meanings.

Textual Notes at the end of the play indicate major departures from the Folio. They take the following form: the reading of our text is given in bold and its source given after an equals sign, with "Q" indicating a Quarto reading, "F2" a reading that derives from the Second Folio of 1632, "F3" from the Third Folio of 1663, and "Ed" that it derives from the subsequent editorial tradition. The rejected Folio ("F") reading is then given. Thus, for example, "**2.3.24 leman** = Ed. F = Lemon" means that at Act 2 Scene 3 lines 23–24, the phrase "I sent thee sixpence for thy Lemon" clearly made little sense and a later editor has concluded that a compositor's (or possibly scribal) error occurred and emended it to "leman," meaning "sweetheart."

KEY FACTS

MAJOR PARTS: (*with percentages of lines/number of speeches/scenes on stage*) Sir Toby Belch (13%/152/10), Viola (13%/121/8), Olivia (12%/118/6), Feste (12%/104/7), Malvolio (11%/87/7), Orsino (9%/59/4), Sir Andrew (6%/88/8), Maria (6%/59/6), Sebastian (5%/31/5), Fabian (4%/51/4), Antonio (4%/26/4).

LINGUISTIC MEDIUM: 40% verse, 60% prose.

DATE: 1601: Performed at Middle Temple February 1602; not mentioned by Meres 1598; alludes to Anthony Sherley's visit to the Persian Sophy (1598–1601) and to a map first published in 1599; parodies the motif of self-love, double title, and use of word "element" in Ben Jonson's *The Fountain of Self-Love, or Cynthia's Revels* (late 1600/early 1601), while a character in Jonson's *Poetaster* (performed later in 1601) seems to say that he has been to a performance of *Twelfth Night*.

SOURCES: Main plot adapted from the story of "Apollonius and Silla" in Barnaby Riche's *Riche his Farewell to Military Profession* (1581), though the motif of the cross-dressed disguised "page" wooing a lady on behalf of a master whom she loves herself is derived from a series of Italian comedies going back to *Gl'Ingannati* ("The Deceived"), an extremely bawdy play performed by "The Academy of the Thunderstruck" in Siena (1537). The mistaking of twins is bred from Plautus' *Menaechmi* by way of Shakespeare's own *Comedy of Errors*. There is no clear source for the Sir Toby/Malvolio plot.

TEXT: First Folio of 1623 is only early printed text. Probably set from scribal copy, it is exceptionally free from errors and textual problems.

TWELFTH NIGHT,
OR WHAT YOU WILL

LIST OF PARTS

ORSINO, Duke of Illyria

CURIO ⎫ courtiers attending
VALENTINE ⎭ upon Orsino

VIOLA, later disguised as Cesario

A Sea-CAPTAIN

SEBASTIAN, Viola's twin brother

ANTONIO, another sea-captain

OLIVIA, a Countess in Illyria

MARIA, her waiting-woman

SIR TOBY **Belch**, Olivia's kinsman

SIR ANDREW **Aguecheek**, companion of Sir Toby

MALVOLIO, Olivia's steward

FABIAN, a member of Olivia's household

FESTE the clown, Olivia's jester

Musicians, Sailors, Lords, Officers, Servants, Attendants, and a Priest

Act 1 Scene 1

Enter Orsino Duke of Illyria, Curio and other Lords   *Music plays*

ORSINO   If music be the food of love, play on,
Give me excess of it, that surfeiting,
The appetite may sicken and so die.
That strain again, it had a dying fall:
5   O, it came o'er my ear like the sweet sound
That breathes upon a bank of violets,
Stealing and giving odour. Enough, no more,
'Tis not so sweet now as it was before.   *Music stops*
O spirit of love, how quick and fresh art thou
10   That, notwithstanding thy capacity,
Receiveth as the sea. Nought enters there,
Of what validity and pitch soe'er,
But falls into abatement and low price
Even in a minute. So full of shapes is fancy
15   That it alone is high fantastical.

CURIO   Will you go hunt, my lord?

ORSINO   What, Curio?

CURIO   The hart.

ORSINO   Why so I do, the noblest that I have.
20   O, when mine eyes did see Olivia first,
Methought she purged the air of pestilence.
That instant was I turned into a hart,

1.1 Location: *Illyria (country on the east of the Adriatic Sea; now Croatia). The entire action takes place here, moving between the households of Duke Orsino and Olivia, with occasional scenes in undetermined public places*   **Orsino** Italian for "bear-cub"; perhaps suggestive of immaturity   **Curio** either "curious" or "courtly" (from the Italian for "court"); may suggest fastidious affectation in dress and manners   **2 surfeiting** overindulging (in food or sex)   **3 appetite** hunger/sexual craving   **4 dying fall** dropping cadence (plays on the sense of "orgasm and detumescence")   **5 sound** i.e. of a breeze   **9 quick and fresh** sharp and eager, hungry   **10 capacity** (small) size/ability to contain   **11 as the sea** i.e. without limit   **12 validity and pitch** worth and utmost elevation   **13 abatement** diminution   **14 shapes** imaginary forms   **fancy** love/desire (plays on the sense of "imagination")   **15 alone . . . fantastical** is uniquely imaginative/delusory   **18 hart** male deer (Orsino puns on "heart")   **21 pestilence** plague (often attributed to bad air)

And my desires, like fell and cruel hounds,
E'er since pursue me.

Enter Valentine

How now, what news from her?

25   **VALENTINE**   So please my lord, I might not be admitted,
But from her handmaid do return this answer:
The element itself, till seven years' heat,
Shall not behold her face at ample view,
But like a cloistress she will veilèd walk,
30   And water once a day her chamber round
With eye-offending brine — all this to season
A brother's dead love, which she would keep fresh
And lasting in her sad remembrance.

  ORSINO   O, she that hath a heart of that fine frame
35   To pay this debt of love but to a brother,
How will she love when the rich golden shaft
Hath killed the flock of all affections else
That live in her — when liver, brain and heart,
These sovereign thrones, are all supplied, and filled
40   Her sweet perfections with one self king!
Away before me, to sweet beds of flowers.
Love thoughts lie rich when canopied with bowers.

Exeunt

Act 1 Scene 2

Enter Viola, a Captain and Sailors

  VIOLA   What country, friends, is this?
  CAPTAIN   This is Illyria, lady.

---

23 fell fierce   **hounds . . . me** as in the classical myth of Actaeon, hunted down by his own hounds as punishment for gazing on the naked goddess Diana   *Valentine* the name of the patron saint of lovers   **27 element** sky   **years' heat** i.e. summers   **28 ample** full, i.e. unveiled   **29 cloistress** nun   **31 eye-offending brine** stinging, salty tears   **season** preserve (with salt)   **36 golden shaft** i.e. arrow of Cupid (god of love)   **37 affections else** other feelings   **38 liver . . . heart** seats (**thrones**) of sexual passion, intellect, and emotion   **39 supplied** filled/satisfied   **filled . . . perfections** her perfect qualities are filled   **40 one self** one and the same   **1.2** *Viola* Italian for "violet," a flower that symbolized faithfulness and was thought to purge melancholy; also suggestive of musical instrument

VIOLA	And what should I do in Illyria?

      My brother he is in Elysium.

5   Perchance he is not drowned: what think you, sailors?

CAPTAIN   It is perchance that you yourself were saved.

VIOLA   O, my poor brother! And so perchance may he be.

CAPTAIN   True, madam, and to comfort you with chance,

      Assure yourself, after our ship did split,

10   When you and those poor number saved with you

      Hung on our driving boat, I saw your brother,

      Most provident in peril, bind himself —

      Courage and hope both teaching him the practice —

      To a strong mast that lived upon the sea,

15   Where, like Arion on the dolphin's back,

      I saw him hold acquaintance with the waves

      So long as I could see.

VIOLA   For saying so, there's gold.   *Gives money*

      Mine own escape unfoldeth to my hope,

20   Whereto thy speech serves for authority,

      The like of him. Know'st thou this country?

CAPTAIN   Ay, madam, well, for I was bred and born

      Not three hours' travel from this very place.

VIOLA   Who governs here?

25   CAPTAIN   A noble duke, in nature as in name.

VIOLA   What is his name?

CAPTAIN   Orsino.

VIOLA   Orsino. I have heard my father name him.

      He was a bachelor then.

30   CAPTAIN   And so is now, or was so very late,

      For but a month ago I went from hence,

      And then 'twas fresh in murmur — as you know,

---

4 Elysium the heaven of classical mythology   **5 Perchance** perhaps (the Captain shifts the
sense to "by chance")   **8 chance** the possibility of good fortune   **11 driving** storm-driven
12 provident foresighted/resourceful/fortunate   **13 practice** method   **14 lived** floated
15 Arion Greek musician who jumped overboard to escape being murdered and was carried to
safety by a dolphin charmed by his music   **16 hold acquaintance with** remain afloat upon
19 unfoldeth . . . hope encourages me to hope   **21 like of him** i.e. that he has also survived
30 late recently   **32 murmur** rumor

What great ones do, the less will prattle of —
That he did seek the love of fair Olivia.

35 VIOLA　What's she?

CAPTAIN　A virtuous maid, the daughter of a count
That died some twelvemonth since, then leaving her
In the protection of his son, her brother,
Who shortly also died, for whose dear love,
40 They say, she hath abjured the sight
And company of men.

VIOLA　O that I served that lady,
And might not be delivered to the world
Till I had made mine own occasion mellow,
45 What my estate is.

CAPTAIN　That were hard to compass,
Because she will admit no kind of suit,
No, not the duke's.

VIOLA　There is a fair behaviour in thee, captain,
50 And though that nature with a beauteous wall
Doth oft close in pollution, yet of thee
I will believe thou hast a mind that suits
With this thy fair and outward character.
I prithee — and I'll pay thee bounteously —
55 Conceal me what I am, and be my aid
For such disguise as haply shall become
The form of my intent. I'll serve this duke.
Thou shalt present me as an eunuch to him.
It may be worth thy pains, for I can sing
60 And speak to him in many sorts of music
That will allow me very worth his service.
What else may hap, to time I will commit,
Only shape thou thy silence to my wit.

---

33 What . . . of whatever the aristocracy do, the lower classes gossip about it　**43 be . . . is** have my identity/rank revealed until I decide the time is ripe　**46 compass** bring about **47 suit** petition/courtship　**48 not** not even　**49 fair behaviour** good conduct/promising appearance　**50 though that** though　**51 close in** enclose　**52 suits With** matches **53 character** appearance　**56 haply . . . intent** may suit the shape of the purpose　**58 eunuch** male castrated to maintain a high singing voice　**61 allow** prove　**worth** worthy of　**62 hap** happen, chance to occur　**63 wit** cunning plan

CAPTAIN	Be you his eunuch, and your mute I'll be:	
65	When my tongue blabs, then let mine eyes not see.	
VIOLA	I thank thee. Lead me on.	

Exeunt

Act 1 Scene 3

Enter Sir Toby [Belch] and Maria

SIR TOBY   What a plague means my niece to take the death of her brother thus? I am sure care's an enemy to life.

MARIA   By my troth, Sir Toby, you must come in earlier a-nights: your cousin, my lady, takes great exceptions to
5   your ill hours.

SIR TOBY   Why, let her except, before excepted.

MARIA   Ay, but you must confine yourself within the modest limits of order.

SIR TOBY   Confine? I'll confine myself no finer than I am:
10   these clothes are good enough to drink in, and so be these boots too. An they be not, let them hang themselves in their own straps.

MARIA   That quaffing and drinking will undo you. I heard my lady talk of it yesterday, and of a foolish knight that you
15   brought in one night here to be her wooer.

SIR TOBY   Who, Sir Andrew Aguecheek?

MARIA   Ay, he.

SIR TOBY   He's as tall a man as any's in Illyria.

MARIA   What's that to th'purpose?

20   SIR TOBY   Why, he has three thousand ducats a year.

1.3   1 What a plague an oath, like "what the hell"   **niece** Toby may be Olivia's uncle, but "niece" could be used more generally for any female relative   **2 care** worry/grief   **3 troth** faith   **4 a-nights** at night   **cousin** relative   **5 ill** antisocial   **6 except, before excepted** plays on the legal phrase *exceptis excipiendis* ("with the aforementioned exceptions"); essentially Sir Toby says he does not care, Olivia may object all she likes   **8 modest** moderate   **9 confine . . . finer** I won't restrain myself further/I won't dress more finely   **11 An** if   **13 quaffing** copious drinking   **16 Aguecheek** suggesting thin face of one suffering from a fever (ague) **18 tall** brave/noble/of great height (Maria understands the latter meaning)   **any's** any (man) is   **20 ducats** gold coins (**three thousand** was a considerable annual income)

MARIA   Ay, but he'll have but a year in all these ducats: he's a very fool and a prodigal.

SIR TOBY   Fie, that you'll say so! He plays o'th'viol-de-gamboys, and speaks three or four languages word for word without book, and hath all the good gifts of nature.

MARIA   He hath indeed, almost natural, for, besides that he's a fool, he's a great quarreller: and but that he hath the gift of a coward to allay the gust he hath in quarrelling, 'tis thought among the prudent he would quickly have the gift of a grave.

SIR TOBY   By this hand, they are scoundrels and subtractors that say so of him. Who are they?

MARIA   They that add, moreover, he's drunk nightly in your company.

SIR TOBY   With drinking healths to my niece. I'll drink to her as long as there is a passage in my throat and drink in Illyria. He's a coward and a coystrill that will not drink to my niece till his brains turn o'th'toe like a parish top. What, wench? *Castiliano vulgo!* For here comes Sir Andrew Agueface.

Enter Sir Andrew [Aguecheek]

SIR ANDREW   Sir Toby Belch. How now, Sir Toby Belch?

SIR TOBY   Sweet Sir Andrew.

SIR ANDREW   Bless you, fair shrew.   *To Maria*

MARIA   And you too, sir.

SIR TOBY   Accost, Sir Andrew, accost.

SIR ANDREW   What's that?

SIR TOBY   My niece's chambermaid.

SIR ANDREW   Good Mistress Accost, I desire better acquaintance.

MARIA   My name is Mary, sir.

---

21 he'll . . . ducats he'll have spent all his money in a year   22 very complete/veritable
prodigal excessively extravagant person   23 o'th'viol-de-gamboys the viol da gamba, a bass
viol played held between the legs (often has sexual connotations)   25 without book i.e.
spontaneously, from memory   26 natural like an idiot   28 allay . . . in reduce his taste for
31 subtractors detractors, slanderers   37 coystrill knave   38 o'th'toe head-over-heels
parish top large spinning-top (kept rotating by being whipped), provided for parishioners'
entertainment   39 *Castiliano vulgo!* unclear Latin-Italian phrase; possibly "Speak of the
devil!"   Agueface playful variation of Aguecheek   42 shrew small mouse/troublesome one
44 Accost approach/woo/grapple with   46 chambermaid female attendant

SIR ANDREW   Good Mistress Mary Accost—

50   SIR TOBY   You mistake, knight. 'Accost' is front her, board her,
woo her, assail her.

SIR ANDREW   By my troth, I would not undertake her in this
company. Is that the meaning of 'accost'?

MARIA   Fare you well, gentlemen.   *Starts to leave*

55   SIR TOBY   An thou let part so, Sir Andrew, would thou mightst
never draw sword again.

SIR ANDREW   An you part so, mistress, I would I might never
draw sword again. Fair lady, do you think you have fools in
hand?

60   MARIA   Sir, I have not you by th'hand.

SIR ANDREW   Marry, but you shall have, and here's   *Gives her his*
my hand.   *hand*

MARIA   Now, sir, thought is free. I pray you bring your hand
to th'buttery-bar and let it drink.

65   SIR ANDREW   Wherefore, sweetheart? What's your metaphor?

MARIA   It's dry, sir.

SIR ANDREW   Why, I think so: I am not such an ass but I can keep
my hand dry. But what's your jest?

MARIA   A dry jest, sir.

70   SIR ANDREW   Are you full of them?

MARIA   Ay, sir, I have them at my fingers'   *Lets go of his hand*
ends.
Marry, now I let go your hand, I am barren.

Exit Maria

---

50 front confront   **board** accost (sexual-naval metaphor referring to sex as attacking a ship)
51 assail attack, seduce   **52 undertake** approach/have sex with (literally, "have her
underneath me")   **in this company** in front of spectators   **55 An . . . so** if you let her leave in
this way   **56 sword** symbol of gentlemanly status (with phallic connotations)   **58 in hand** to
deal with (Maria takes the phrase literally; also plays on the idea of masturbation)   **61 Marry**
by the virgin Mary   **63 thought is free** think what you like (proverbial)   **64 th'buttery-bar**
the ledge created by opening the half-door of the buttery, with play on genitals   **65 Wherefore**
why   **66 dry** thirsty/shriveled/impotent (supposedly signified by a dry palm)   **67 I . . . dry**
alludes to the proverb "fools have wit enough to come in out of the rain"   **69 dry jest** stupid/
ironic   **71 at . . . ends** always ready/literally by the hand   **72 barren** empty of jests and of Sir
Andrew's hand

SIR TOBY   O knight, thou lack'st a cup of canary. When did I see thee so put down?

75 SIR ANDREW   Never in your life, I think, unless you see canary put me down. Methinks sometimes I have no more wit than a Christian or an ordinary man has. But I am a great eater of beef and I believe that does harm to my wit.

SIR TOBY   No question.

80 SIR ANDREW   An I thought that, I'd forswear it. I'll ride home tomorrow, Sir Toby.

SIR TOBY   *Pourquoi*, my dear knight?

SIR ANDREW   What is '*Pourquoi*'? Do or not do? I would I had bestowed that time in the tongues that I have in fencing, 85 dancing and bear-baiting. O, had I but followed the arts!

SIR TOBY   Then hadst thou had an excellent head of hair.

SIR ANDREW   Why, would that have mended my hair?

SIR TOBY   Past question, for thou see'st it will not curl by nature.

90 SIR ANDREW   But it becomes me well enough, does't not?

SIR TOBY   Excellent. It hangs like flax on a distaff, and I hope to see a housewife take thee between her legs and spin it off.

SIR ANDREW   Faith, I'll home tomorrow, Sir Toby. Your niece will not be seen, or if she be, it's four to one she'll none of me. The 95 count himself here hard by woos her.

SIR TOBY   She'll none o'th'count. She'll not match above her degree, neither in estate, years, nor wit; I have heard her swear't. Tut, there's life in't, man.

---

73 **canary** sweet wine from the Canary Islands; also continues play on impotence   **74 put down** snubbed (Sir Andrew plays on the senses of "drunk/impotent")   **77 Christian** i.e. average man   **eater . . . wit** beef was thought to dull the intellect; **wit** may also signify "penis" and **beef** "whore," implying impotence as a result of veneral disease   **80 forswear it** give it up   **82 *Pourquoi*** "why" (French)   **84 tongues** foreign languages   **85 bear-baiting** spectator sport in which a bear chained to a stake was attacked by dogs   **the arts** liberal arts/academic learning   **86 head of hair** puns on **tongues** pronounced "tongs," thus suggesting a barber's curling tongs   **87 mended** improved   **90 becomes** suits   **91 flax** yellow fiber   **distaff** staff used to spin flax   **92 housewife** woman who keeps house/prostitute   **take . . . off** treat Sir Andrew as a distaff and his hair as flax to be spun/have sex with Sir Andrew, resulting in syphilitic hair loss   **94 none of me** have nothing to do with me   **95 count** i.e. Duke Orsino   **hard** near   **97 degree** (social) position   **estate** status/fortune   **wit** intelligence   **98 life in't** still hope (proverbial)

SIR ANDREW   I'll stay a month longer. I am a fellow o'th'
strangest mind i'th'world: I delight in masques and revels
sometimes altogether.

SIR TOBY   Art thou good at these kickshawses, knight?

SIR ANDREW   As any man in Illyria, whatsoever he be, under the
degree of my betters, and yet I will not compare with an old
man.

SIR TOBY   What is thy excellence in a galliard, knight?

SIR ANDREW   Faith, I can cut a caper.

SIR TOBY   And I can cut the mutton to't.

SIR ANDREW   And I think I have the back-trick simply as strong
as any man in Illyria.

SIR TOBY   Wherefore are these things hid? Wherefore have
these gifts a curtain before 'em? Are they like to take dust,
like Mistress Mall's picture? Why dost thou not go to church
in a galliard and come home in a coranto? My very walk
should be a jig, I would not so much as make water but in a
sink-a-pace. What dost thou mean? Is it a world to hide
virtues in? I did think, by the excellent constitution of thy
leg, it was formed under the star of a galliard.

SIR ANDREW   Ay, 'tis strong, and it does indifferent well in a
damned coloured stock. Shall we set about some revels?

SIR TOBY   What shall we do else? Were we not born under
Taurus?

SIR ANDREW   Taurus? That's sides and heart.

---

100 strangest oddest/most extraordinary   masques and revels courtly entertainments
involving dancing   102 kickshawses trivial distractions/sexual sweetmeats   103 under . . .
betters except for my social superiors   104 old man expert   106 galliard lively dance
107 cut a caper perform a leap/have sex   108 cut . . . to't plays on the sense of caper as a
berry used in sauce for mutton; also a prostitute   109 back-trick backward dance step/sex
112 like to take likely to gather   113 Mistress Mall's picture i.e. a portrait protected from dust
and light by a curtain (Mall is a diminutive of "Mary")   114 in doing   coranto running
dance   115 jig rapid, springing dance   make water urinate   116 sink-a-pace cinquepace, a
lively dance with five steps; may play on the sense of sink as "sewer"   117 virtues talents
118 star . . . galliard astrological influence favorable to dancing   119 indifferent moderately
120 damned damnably (the Folio reading "dam'd" is defensible as an intensifier, but it could be
emended to, e.g., "damson-coloured" or "flame-coloured")   stock stocking   123 Taurus . . .
heart zodiacal signs were thought to govern parts of the body

SIR TOBY   No, sir, it is legs and thighs. Let me see   *Sir Andrew*
125   thee caper. Ha? Higher, ha, ha! Excellent!   *Exeunt*   *dances*

Act 1 Scene 4

running scene 4

Enter Valentine and Viola [as Cesario] in man's attire

VALENTINE   If the duke continue these favours towards you,
Cesario, you are like to be much advanced. He hath known
you but three days, and already you are no stranger.

VIOLA   You either fear his humour or my negligence, that
5   you call in question the continuance of his love. Is he
inconstant, sir, in his favours?

VALENTINE   No, believe me.

Enter Duke [Orsino], Curio and Attendants

VIOLA   I thank you. Here comes the count.

ORSINO   Who saw Cesario, ho?

10   VIOLA   On your attendance, my lord, here.

ORSINO   Stand you awhile aloof.— Cesario,   *To Attendants, who*
Thou know'st no less but all. I have unclasped   *stand aside*
To thee the book even of my secret soul:
Therefore, good youth, address thy gait unto her,
15   Be not denied access, stand at her doors,
And tell them there thy fixèd foot shall grow
Till thou have audience.

VIOLA   Sure, my noble lord,
If she be so abandoned to her sorrow
20   As it is spoke, she never will admit me.

ORSINO   Be clamorous and leap all civil bounds
Rather than make unprofited return.

VIOLA   Say I do speak with her, my lord, what then?

---

124 **legs and thighs** more usually Taurus was said to govern the neck and throat
1.4   2 Cesario suggests "little Caesar" and perhaps the idea of splitting/separating (as in
"Cesarean" and "caesura")   **advanced** promoted   **4 humour** disposition/capriciousness
10 On your attendance ready to serve you   **11 aloof** to one side   **12 no . . . all** i.e. everything
14 address thy gait direct your steps   **16 them** i.e. Olivia's servants   **grow** i.e. take root
17 audience reception by Olivia   **20 spoke** said, rumored   **21 civil bounds** bounds of
civilized behavior

ORSINO   O, then unfold the passion of my love,
25   Surprise her with discourse of my dear faith;
        It shall become thee well to act my woes.
        She will attend it better in thy youth
        Than in a nuncio's of more grave aspect.
VIOLA   I think not so, my lord.
30   ORSINO   Dear lad, believe it;
        For they shall yet belie thy happy years,
        That say thou art a man: Diana's lip
        Is not more smooth and rubious, thy small pipe
        Is as the maiden's organ, shrill and sound,
35   And all is semblative a woman's part.
        I know thy constellation is right apt
        For this affair.— Some four or five attend him.   *To Attendants*
        All, if you will, for I myself am best
        When least in company. Prosper well in this,
40   And thou shalt live as freely as thy lord,
        To call his fortunes thine.
VIOLA   I'll do my best
        To woo your lady.— Yet, a barful strife!   *Aside*
        Whoe'er I woo, myself would be his wife.   *Exeunt*

Act 1 Scene 5   *running scene 5*

Enter Maria and Clown [Feste]

MARIA   Nay, either tell me where thou hast been, or I will
        not open my lips so wide as a bristle may enter in way of thy
        excuse. My lady will hang thee for thy absence.

---

25 Surprise ambush, take unawares   **faith** faithful love   **26 become** suit   **27 attend** listen,
pay attention to   **28 nuncio's** messenger's   **aspect** appearance   **30 lad** servant/young man
31 belie deceive   **32 Diana's lip** Diana was the Roman goddess of the moon, hunting, and
chastity; in view of "pipe" and "organ," **lip** may play on "nether lip" (labia)   **33 rubious** ruby
red   **pipe** voice/penis   **34 shrill and sound** high-pitched and unbroken   **35 is semblative**
resembles   **part** attributes/role/sexual **organ**   **36 constellation** disposition determined by the
stars   **40 freely** independently   **43 barful strife** effort full of hindrances   **1.5**   *Feste* From
Latin or Italian, *festa* ("feast" or "festival"), an appropriate name for a fool/clown   **2 in** by

FESTE	Let her hang me: he that is well hanged in this world	
5	needs to fear no colours.	
MARIA	Make that good.	
FESTE	He shall see none to fear.	
MARIA	A good lenten answer. I can tell thee where that saying was born, of 'I fear no colours.'	
10 FESTE	Where, good Mistress Mary?	
MARIA	In the wars, and that may you be bold to say in your foolery.	
FESTE	Well, God give them wisdom that have it, and those that are fools, let them use their talents.	
15 MARIA	Yet you will be hanged for being so long absent, or, to be turned away, is not that as good as a hanging to you?	
FESTE	Many a good hanging prevents a bad marriage, and, for turning away, let summer bear it out.	
MARIA	You are resolute, then?	
20 FESTE	Not so, neither. But I am resolved on two points.	
MARIA	That if one break, the other will hold, or if both break, your gaskins fall.	
FESTE	Apt, in good faith, very apt. Well, go thy way. If Sir Toby would leave drinking, thou wert as witty a piece of	
25	Eve's flesh as any in Illyria.	
MARIA	Peace, you rogue, no more o'that. Here comes my lady: make your excuse wisely, you were best. *[Exit]*	

Enter Lady Olivia with Malvolio [and Attendants]

FESTE	Wit, an't be thy will, put me into good *Aside*	
	fooling! Those wits, that think they have thee, do very oft	

---

4 **well hanged** plays on the sense of "with a large penis"   5 **no colours** i.e. nothing (literally, military flags); puns on "collars" (nooses)   6 **Make that good** justify yourself   7 **He . . . fear** i.e. a dead man cannot see (enemy **colours**)   8 **lenten** meager (Lent, the time of fasting, was especially associated with puritanism)   11 **bold** confident/certain   16 **turned away** dismissed from service   17 **Many . . . marriage** proverbial; **good hanging** may continue play on the sense of "large penis"   18 **for** as for   **let . . . out** i.e. good weather will make dismissal more bearable   20 **points** matters (Maria plays on the sense of "laces used to hold up breeches")   22 **gaskins** breeches   23 **Apt** quick, witty   **If . . . drinking** either never, or suggesting that Maria and Sir Toby would be a good match   25 **Eve's flesh** woman   27 **were best** are best advised   *Malvolio* "ill-will" (Latin)   28 **an't** if it

30   prove fools, and I that am sure I lack thee, may pass for a wise
          man. For what says Quinapalus? 'Better a witty fool than a
          foolish wit.'— God bless thee, lady.   *To Olivia*

OLIVIA   Take the fool away.   *To Attendants*

FESTE   Do you not hear, fellows? Take away the lady.

35 OLIVIA   Go to, you're a dry fool. I'll no more of you. Besides,
          you grow dishonest.

FESTE   Two faults, Madonna, that drink and good counsel
          will amend. For give the dry fool drink, then is the fool not
          dry: bid the dishonest man mend himself. If he mend, he is
40   no longer dishonest; if he cannot, let the botcher mend him.
          Anything that's mended is but patched: virtue that
          transgresses is but patched with sin, and sin that amends is
          but patched with virtue. If that this simple syllogism will
          serve, so. If it will not, what remedy? As there is no true
45   cuckold but calamity, so beauty's a flower. The lady bade
          take away the fool: therefore, I say again, take her away.

OLIVIA   Sir, I bade them take away you.

FESTE   Misprision in the highest degree! Lady, *cucullus non
          facit monachum*: that's as much to say as I wear not motley in
50   my brain. Good madonna, give me leave to prove you a fool.

OLIVIA   Can you do it?

FESTE   Dexteriously, good madonna.

OLIVIA   Make your proof.

---

31 Quinapalus an invented authority, perhaps playing on French *qui n'a pas lu* ("unread") or
mock Italian "him on the stick" (the face on the fool's bauble)   **35 Go to** expression of
impatient dismissal   **dry** dull   **36 dishonest** undutiful   **37 Madonna** "my lady" (Italian)
39 dry dull/thirsty   **mend** improve; later plays on the sense of "repair"   **40 botcher** mender
of clothes and shoes   **41 patched** simply mended, covered up; also alludes to the fool's
multicolored costume   **43 simple** uncomplicated/foolish   **syllogism** reasoning based on two
premises (here those concerning virtue and sin)   **44 so** well and good   **no . . . calamity** i.e.
one married to calamity will always be faithless   **45 cuckold** man with an unfaithful wife
beauty's a flower i.e. it will fade; Feste advises Olivia to make the most of her youth and beauty,
rather than shutting herself away and refusing to marry   **48 Misprision** error/wrongful
arrest   *cucullus . . . monachum* "a hood does not make a monk" (Latin)   **49 motley**
multicolored clothing worn by professional fools   **50 leave** permission   **52 Dexteriously**
skillfully

FESTE   I must catechize you for it, madonna. Good my
55   mouse of virtue, answer me.

OLIVIA   Well, sir, for want of other idleness, I'll bide your
proof.

FESTE   Good madonna, why mourn'st thou?

OLIVIA   Good fool, for my brother's death.

60   FESTE   I think his soul is in hell, madonna.

OLIVIA   I know his soul is in heaven, fool.

FESTE   The more fool, madonna, to mourn for your
brother's soul being in heaven. Take away the fool,
gentlemen.

65   OLIVIA   What think you of this fool, Malvolio? Doth he not
mend?

MALVOLIO   Yes, and shall do till the pangs of death shake him.
Infirmity, that decays the wise, doth ever make the better
fool.

70   FESTE   God send you, sir, a speedy infirmity, for the better
increasing your folly! Sir Toby will be sworn that I am no fox,
but he will not pass his word for twopence that you are no
fool.

OLIVIA   How say you to that, Malvolio?

75   MALVOLIO   I marvel your ladyship takes delight in such a
barren rascal. I saw him put down the other day with an
ordinary fool that has no more brain than a stone. Look you
now, he's out of his guard already. Unless you laugh and
minister occasion to him, he is gagged. I protest, I take these
80   wise men, that crow so at these set kind of fools, no better
than the fools' zanies.

---

54 catechize cross-examine (literally, form of Church instruction in which a person answers
a set of questions about the Christian faith)   **Good . . . virtue** my good virtuous mouse;
playful term of endearment   **56 idleness** pastime   **bide** await/endure   **66 mend** improve
(Malvolio shifts the sense to "grow (more foolish)"   **71 no fox** not cunning   **72 pass** give
76 barren dull-witted   **put down** defeated   **with** by   **77 ordinary fool** unexceptional
fool/fool performing at an inn (**ordinary**)/natural idiot   **stone** may also refer to Stone, an
Elizabethan tavern fool   **78 out . . . guard** defenseless (fencing term), i.e. lacking a witty reply
79 minister occasion provide opportunity (for fooling)   **protest** declare   **80 crow** laugh
raucously   **set** unspontaneous   **81 zanies** assistants

OLIVIA   O, you are sick of self-love, Malvolio, and taste with
a distempered appetite. To be generous, guiltless and of free
disposition is to take those things for bird-bolts that you
85   deem cannon-bullets. There is no slander in an allowed fool,
though he do nothing but rail; nor no railing in a known
discreet man, though he do nothing but reprove.

FESTE   Now Mercury endue thee with leasing, for thou
speak'st well of fools.

Enter Maria

90   MARIA   Madam, there is at the gate a young gentleman
much desires to speak with you.

OLIVIA   From the Count Orsino, is it?

MARIA   I know not, madam. 'Tis a fair young man, and well
attended.

95   OLIVIA   Who of my people hold him in delay?

MARIA   Sir Toby, madam, your kinsman.

OLIVIA   Fetch him off, I pray you. He speaks nothing but
madman. Fie on him!—   [*Exit Maria*]
Go you, Malvolio; if it be a suit from the count, I am sick, or
100   not at home. What you will, to dismiss it.—   *Exit Malvolio*
Now you see, sir, how your fooling grows old, and people
dislike it.

FESTE   Thou hast spoke for us, madonna, as if thy eldest
son should be a fool, whose skull Jove cram with brains,
105   for — here he comes —

Enter Sir Toby

one of thy kin has a most weak pia mater.

OLIVIA   By mine honour, half drunk.—   *To Sir Toby*
What is he at the gate, cousin?

---

82 **of** with   83 **distempered** unbalanced   **free** generous   84 **bird-bolts** blunt arrows for
shooting birds   85 **allowed** licensed   86 **rail** rant   87 **discreet** prudent   **reprove** express
disapproval   88 **Mercury . . . leasing** may **Mercury**, god of deception, make you good at lying
98 **madman** i.e. rubbish, gibberish   **Fie** expression of impatience or disgust   100 **What you
will** whatever you want to say   101 **old** stale   104 **should be** were   **Jove** Roman king of the
gods   106 **pia mater** brain (literally, soft membrane enclosing it)

SIR TOBY	A gentleman.	
110 OLIVIA	A gentleman? What gentleman?	
SIR TOBY	'Tis a gentleman here—	*Belches/To Feste*

SIR TOBY 'Tis a gentleman here—   *Belches/To Feste*
a plague o'these pickle herring!— How now, sot?

FESTE   Good Sir Toby!

OLIVIA   Cousin, cousin, how have you come so early by this
115   lethargy?

SIR TOBY   Lechery? I defy lechery. There's one at the gate.

OLIVIA   Ay, marry, what is he?

SIR TOBY   Let him be the devil, an he will, I care not. Give me
faith, say I. Well, it's all one.   *Exit*

120   OLIVIA   What's a drunken man like, fool?

FESTE   Like a drowned man, a fool and a madman: one
draught above heat makes him a fool, the second mads him,
and a third drowns him.

OLIVIA   Go thou and seek the crowner, and let him sit o'my
125   coz, for he's in the third degree of drink: he's drowned. Go
look after him.

FESTE   He is but mad yet, madonna, and the fool shall look
to the madman.   *[Exit]*

Enter Malvolio

MALVOLIO   Madam, yond young fellow swears he will speak
130   with you. I told him you were sick, he takes on him to
understand so much, and therefore comes to speak with
you. I told him you were asleep — he seems to have a
foreknowledge of that too — and therefore comes to speak
with you. What is to be said to him, lady? He's fortified
135   against any denial.

OLIVIA   Tell him he shall not speak with me.

112 sot fool/drunkard   115 lethargy (drunken) state   116 one someone   119 faith i.e. to
defy the devil   it's all one it doesn't matter   121 one . . . heat one drink beyond that which
would warm him   123 drowns makes him excessively drunk/unintelligible/unconscious
124 crowner coroner   sit o'my coz hold an inquest on my kinsman   129 yond yonder, that
130 takes . . . understand understands

MALVOLIO   He's been told so, and he says he'll stand at your
door like a sheriff's post, and be the supporter to a bench, but
he'll speak with you.

140 OLIVIA   What kind o'man is he?

MALVOLIO   Why, of mankind.

OLIVIA   What manner of man?

MALVOLIO   Of very ill manner. He'll speak with you, will you
or no.

145 OLIVIA   Of what personage and years is he?

MALVOLIO   Not yet old enough for a man, nor young enough
for a boy. As a squash is before 'tis a peascod, or a codling
when 'tis almost an apple: 'tis with him in standing water,
between boy and man. He is very well-favoured and he
150 speaks very shrewishly. One would think his mother's milk
were scarce out of him.

OLIVIA   Let him approach. Call in my gentlewoman.

MALVOLIO   Gentlewoman, my lady calls.   *Exit*

Enter Maria

OLIVIA   Give me my veil. Come, throw it o'er my face. We'll
155 once more hear Orsino's embassy.   *She is veiled*

Enter Viola [and Attendants]

VIOLA   The honourable lady of the house, which is she?

OLIVIA   Speak to me, I shall answer for her. Your will?

VIOLA   Most radiant, exquisite and unmatchable beauty —
I pray you tell me if this be the lady of the house, for I never
160 saw her. I would be loath to cast away my speech, for besides
that it is excellently well penned, I have taken great pains to
con it. Good beauties, let me sustain no scorn; I am very
comptible, even to the least sinister usage.

---

138 sheriff's post decorated post denoting authority, fixed in front of the sheriff's door
supporter . . . bench furniture support (**bench** plays on the sense of "court of justice")
141 of mankind i.e. ordinary   **143 ill manner** i.e. impolite   **will . . . no** whether you want to
or not   **145 personage** appearance   **147 squash** unripe pea-pod (**peascod,** allusive of
genitals—a humorous reversal of "codpiece," a bag worn over the opening at the front of a
man's breeches)   **codling** unripe apple, plays on "cod" meaning "scrotum"   **148 standing
water** at the turn of the tide   **149 well-favoured** good-looking   **150 shrewishly** sharply/
shrilly   **155 embassy** message/ambassador   **160 cast away** waste   **161 penned** written
162 con learn by heart   **sustain** endure   **163 comptible** sensitive   **sinister** impolite

OLIVIA   Whence came you, sir?

165 VIOLA   I can say little more than I have studied, and that question's out of my part. Good gentle one, give me modest assurance, if you be the lady of the house, that I may proceed in my speech.

OLIVIA   Are you a comedian?

170 VIOLA   No, my profound heart. And yet, by the very fangs of malice, I swear I am not that I play. Are you the lady of the house?

OLIVIA   If I do not usurp myself, I am.

VIOLA   Most certain, if you are she, you do usurp yourself,
175   for what is yours to bestow is not yours to reserve. But this is from my commission. I will on with my speech in your praise, and then show you the heart of my message.

OLIVIA   Come to what is important in't. I forgive you the praise.

180 VIOLA   Alas, I took great pains to study it, and 'tis poetical.

OLIVIA   It is the more like to be feigned. I pray you keep it in. I heard you were saucy at my gates, and allowed your approach rather to wonder at you than to hear you. If you be not mad, be gone. If you have reason, be brief. 'Tis not that
185   time of moon with me to make one in so skipping a dialogue.

MARIA   Will you hoist sail, sir? Here lies your way.

VIOLA   No, good swabber, I am to hull here a little longer. Some mollification for your giant, sweet lady; tell me your mind, I am a messenger.

---

165 studied learned, memorized   **166 out . . . part** not within my brief   **modest** reasonable
169 comedian actor   **170 my profound heart** upon my soul/(to Olivia) my wise lady
171 that I play the character I perform   **173 usurp** counterfeit (Viola shifts the sense to
"assume unjust authority over")   **175 what . . . reserve** i.e. Olivia should not withhold herself
from love and marriage   **176 from** outside, not part of   **on** go on   **178 forgive** excuse from
repeating   **181 feigned** fictional/insincere   **it in** in it to yourself   **182 saucy** impudent
183 wonder marvel   **184 If . . . brief** i.e. if Viola has any sense at all she should go; any
sensible message must be conveyed quickly   **'Tis . . . me** I am not a lunatic, i.e. not affected by
the moon's changes   **185 make one** take part   **skipping** frivolous, mad   **186 hoist sail** i.e.
prepare to leave   **187 swabber** sailor who washes the deck   **hull** float, with sails furled
188 Some mollification please pacify/I have pacified   **giant** i.e. Maria; a joke about Maria's
small size and/or Maria resembles a giant in a romance tale who guarded a lady

190 OLIVIA   Sure, you have some hideous matter to deliver, when the courtesy of it is so fearful. Speak your office.

VIOLA   It alone concerns your ear. I bring no overture of war, no taxation of homage; I hold the olive in my hand. My words are as full of peace as matter.

195 OLIVIA   Yet you began rudely. What are you? What would you?

VIOLA   The rudeness that hath appeared in me have I learned from my entertainment. What I am, and what I would, are as secret as maidenhead: to your ears, divinity: to

200 any other's, profanation.

OLIVIA   Give us the place alone. We will hear this divinity.

[*Exeunt Maria and Attendants*]

Now, sir, what is your text?

VIOLA   Most sweet lady—

OLIVIA   A comfortable doctrine, and much may be said of it.

205 Where lies your text?

VIOLA   In Orsino's bosom.

OLIVIA   In his bosom? In what chapter of his bosom?

VIOLA   To answer by the method, in the first of his heart.

OLIVIA   O, I have read it: it is heresy. Have you no more to

210 say?

VIOLA   Good madam, let me see your face.

OLIVIA   Have you any commission from your lord to negotiate with my face? You are now out of your text. But we will draw the curtain and show you the picture.   *Unveils*

215 Look you, sir, such a one I was this present. Is't not well done?

---

191 **courtesy** introduction, preamble/etiquette   **fearful** frightening, alarming   **Speak your office** perform your task, deliver your speech   192 **overture** disclosure   193 **taxation of homage** demand for money on behalf on a superior lord   **olive** olive branch, symbol of peace   194 **matter** real substance   195 **rudely** i.e. by being saucy at the gates   198 **entertainment** reception   199 **maidenhead** virginity   **divinity** sacred   200 **profanation** blasphemy   202 **text** theme/topic drawn from the Bible for discussion in a sermon   204 **comfortable** comforting   206 **bosom** heart   207 **chapter** as of the Bible   208 **answer . . . method** continue the metaphor   213 **out of** straying from   214 **curtain** i.e. veil covering Olivia's face (**picture**)   215 **such . . . present** i.e. here I am (Olivia speaks of her face as if it was a recent portrait)

VIOLA	Excellently done, if God did all.
OLIVIA	'Tis in grain, sir, 'twill endure wind and weather.
VIOLA	'Tis beauty truly blent, whose red and white

220   Nature's own sweet and cunning hand laid on.
                  Lady, you are the cruell'st she alive,
                  If you will lead these graces to the grave
                  And leave the world no copy.

OLIVIA   O, sir, I will not be so hard-hearted. I will give out
225   divers schedules of my beauty. It shall be inventoried, and
every particle and utensil labelled to my will: as, *item*, two
lips, indifferent red: *item*, two grey eyes, with lids to them:
item, one neck, one chin and so forth. Were you sent hither
to praise me?

230   VIOLA   I see you what you are, you are too proud.
                  But if you were the devil, you are fair.
                  My lord and master loves you. O, such love
                  Could be but recompensed, though you were crowned
                  The nonpareil of beauty!

235   OLIVIA   How does he love me?

VIOLA   With adorations, fertile tears,
                  With groans that thunder love, with sighs of fire.

OLIVIA   Your lord does know my mind: I cannot love him.
                  Yet I suppose him virtuous, know him noble,
240   Of great estate, of fresh and stainless youth;
                  In voices well divulged, free, learned and valiant,
                  And in dimension and the shape of nature
                  A gracious person; but yet I cannot love him.
                  He might have took his answer long ago.

---

217 if . . . all i.e. if all Olivia's beauty is natural, rather than cosmetic or touched up by the metaphorical painter   **218 in grain** indelible, i.e. all natural   **219 truly blent** genuinely blended/realistically painted   **red and white** i.e. lips (or rosy cheeks) and skin   **220 cunning** skillful   **221 she** lady   **222 graces** beauties   **223 copy** replica in the form of a child (Olivia plays on the sense of "list")   **225 divers schedules** several inventories   **inventoried** itemized   **226 utensil** article, feature   **227 indifferent** adequately   **229 praise** puns on "appraise," i.e. evaluate   **231 if** even if   **233 but recompensed, though** no more than repaid, even if **234 nonpareil** paragon   **236 fertile** abundant   **239 suppose** consider   **241 In . . . divulged** well regarded in popular opinion   **free** honorable/generous   **242 dimension . . . nature** physical form   **243 gracious** graceful, attractive

245 VIOLA   If I did love you in my master's flame,
                With such a suff'ring, such a deadly life,
                In your denial I would find no sense,
                I would not understand it.

     OLIVIA   Why, what would you?

250 VIOLA   Make me a willow cabin at your gate,
                And call upon my soul within the house,
                Write loyal cantons of contemnèd love
                And sing them loud even in the dead of night,
                Hallow your name to the reverberate hills

255   And make the babbling gossip of the air
                Cry out 'Olivia!' O, you should not rest
                Between the elements of air and earth,
                But you should pity me!

     OLIVIA   You might do much. What is your parentage?

260 VIOLA   Above my fortunes, yet my state is well:
                I am a gentleman.

     OLIVIA   Get you to your lord.
                I cannot love him. Let him send no more,
                Unless, perchance, you come to me again,

265   To tell me how he takes it. Fare you well:
                I thank you for your pains. Spend this for me.   *Offers a purse*

     VIOLA   I am no fee'd post, lady; keep your purse.
                My master, not myself, lacks recompense.
                Love make his heart of flint that you shall love,

270   And let your fervour, like my master's, be
                Placed in contempt! Farewell, fair cruelty.   *Exit*

     OLIVIA   'What is your parentage?'
                'Above my fortunes, yet my state is well;
                I am a gentleman.' I'll be sworn thou art.

---

245 flame passion   **246 deadly** death-like   **250 willow cabin** shelter made from willow
branches, a symbol of unrequited love   **251 my soul** i.e. Olivia   **252 cantons** songs
contemnèd despised, rejected   **254 Hallow** shout/bless   **reverberate** echoing
255 babbling . . . air like that of Echo, whose unrequited love for Narcissus meant she
wasted away to a mere voice   **gossip** chatter   **260 fortunes** position as a servant
state social status   **well** satisfactory   **267 fee'd post** hired messenger   **269 Love . . . love**
may Love harden the heart of whomever you fall in love with

275   Thy tongue, thy face, thy limbs, actions and spirit,

        Do give thee five-fold blazon. Not too fast. Soft, soft!

        Unless the master were the man. How now?

        Even so quickly may one catch the plague?

        Methinks I feel this youth's perfections

280   With an invisible and subtle stealth

        To creep in at mine eyes. Well, let it be.

        What ho, Malvolio!

Enter Malvolio

MALVOLIO   Here, madam, at your service.

OLIVIA   Run after that same peevish messenger,

285   The county's man. He left this ring behind him,   *Gives a ring*

        Would I or not. Tell him I'll none of it.

        Desire him not to flatter with his lord,

        Nor hold him up with hopes. I am not for him.

        If that the youth will come this way tomorrow,

290   I'll give him reasons for't. Hie thee, Malvolio.

MALVOLIO   Madam, I will.   *Exit*

OLIVIA   I do I know not what, and fear to find

        Mine eye too great a flatterer for my mind.

        Fate, show thy force. Ourselves we do not owe.

295   What is decreed must be, and be this so.   *[Exit]*

Act 2 Scene 1   *running scene 6*

Enter Antonio and Sebastian

ANTONIO   Will you stay no longer? Nor will you not that I go
with you?

SEBASTIAN   By your patience, no. My stars shine darkly over me;

---

276 **blazon** heraldic coat of arms, which could only be displayed by a gentleman   **Soft** wait a
moment   277 **the . . . man** i.e. Orsino and Cesario could change places   **man** servant
278 **catch the plague** i.e. fall in love   284 **peevish** headstrong   285 **county's** count's, i.e.
Duke Orsino's   286 **Would I** whether I wanted it   287 **Desire** ask   **flatter with** i.e. encourage
288 **hold . . . hopes** sustain him with false expectations   290 **Hie** hasten   293 **Mine . . .
mind** my eyes (through which love enters) may have betrayed my reason   294 **owe** own
2.1   1 **Nor . . . not** do you not wish   3 **patience** permission   **darkly** ominously

the malignancy of my fate might perhaps distemper yours;
5   therefore I shall crave of you your leave that I may bear my
evils alone. It were a bad recompense for your love to lay any
of them on you.

ANTONIO   Let me yet know of you whither you are bound.

SEBASTIAN   No, sooth, sir: my determinate voyage is mere
10   extravagancy. But I perceive in you so excellent a touch of
modesty that you will not extort from me what I am willing
to keep in. Therefore it charges me in manners the rather to
express myself. You must know of me then, Antonio, my
name is Sebastian, which I called Roderigo. My father was
15   that Sebastian of Messaline whom I know you have heard of.
He left behind him myself and a sister, both born in an hour.
If the heavens had been pleased, would we had so ended. But
you, sir, altered that, for some hour before you took me from
the breach of the sea was my sister drowned.

20   ANTONIO   Alas the day!

SEBASTIAN   A lady, sir, though it was said she much resembled
me, was yet of many accounted beautiful. But though I
could not with such estimable wonder overfar believe that,
yet thus far I will boldly publish her: she bore a mind that
25   envy could not but call fair. She is drowned already, sir, with
salt water, though I seem to drown her remembrance again
with more.

ANTONIO   Pardon me, sir, your bad entertainment.

SEBASTIAN   O, good Antonio, forgive me your trouble.

---

4 **malignancy** evil influence   **distemper** spoil, unbalance   5 **crave** entreat   **leave**
permission   6 **evils** misfortunes   9 **sooth** (in) truth   **determinate** intended
10 **extravagancy** wandering   11 **modesty** propriety   **am . . . in** wish to keep secret
12 **it . . . manners** politeness compels me   13 **express** reveal   14 **called** said was
15 **Messaline** unclear, possibly Marseilles or Messina, or invented by Shakespeare
16 **an hour** the same hour (they are twins)   18 **some** about an   19 **breach** breaking waves
23 **estimable wonder** admiring judgment   **overfar** too greatly   24 **publish** speak openly
of/celebrate   25 **envy** malice   27 **more** i.e. tears   28 **entertainment** reception (for one so
worthy)   29 **your trouble** the trouble I put you to

30 **ANTONIO**   If you will not murder me for my love, let me be your
          servant.

SEBASTIAN   If you will not undo what you have done, that is, kill
          him whom you have recovered, desire it not. Fare ye well at
          once. My bosom is full of kindness, and I am yet so near the
35   manners of my mother that upon the least occasion more
          mine eyes will tell tales of me. I am bound to the Count
          Orsino's court. Farewell.   *Exit*

ANTONIO   The gentleness of all the gods go with thee!
          I have many enemies in Orsino's court,
40   Else would I very shortly see thee there.
          But come what may, I do adore thee so,
          That danger shall seem sport, and I will go.   *Exit*

Act 2 Scene 2   *running scene 7*

Enter Viola and Malvolio at several doors

MALVOLIO   Were not you ev'n now with the Countess Olivia?

VIOLA   Even now, sir, on a moderate pace I have since
          arrived but hither.

MALVOLIO   She returns this ring to you, sir. You   *Shows a ring*
5   might have saved me my pains, to have taken it away
          yourself. She adds, moreover, that you should put your lord
          into a desperate assurance she will none of him. And one
          thing more, that you be never so hardy to come again in his
          affairs, unless it be to report your lord's taking of this.
10   Receive it so.

VIOLA   She took the ring of me. I'll none of it.

---

30 **murder . . . love** i.e. by making me leave you   33 **recovered** rescued, brought back to life
34 **kindness** tenderness/natural affection (for my sister)   **yet** still   35 **manners . . . mother**
i.e. a womanish inclination to weep   36 **tell . . . me** i.e. betray my feelings by crying
38 **gentleness** good favor   40 **Else** otherwise   42 **sport** recreation   2.2   1 **ev'n** just
2 **on** at   3 **but hither** only this far   7 **desperate assurance** hopeless certainty   8 **hardy** bold
in his affairs on his business   9 **taking of this** understanding of this message/reception of the
ring   10 **it** the ring

MALVOLIO   Come, sir, you peevishly threw it to her, and her will
is, it should be so returned. If it be worth   *Throws it on*
stooping for, there it lies in your eye. If not, be   *the ground*
15   it his that finds it.   *Exit*

VIOLA   I left no ring with her. What means this lady?
Fortune forbid my outside have not charmed her!
She made good view of me, indeed so much
That methought her eyes had lost her tongue,
20   For she did speak in starts distractedly.
She loves me, sure. The cunning of her passion
Invites me in this churlish messenger.
None of my lord's ring? Why, he sent her none;
I am the man. If it be so, as 'tis,
25   Poor lady, she were better love a dream.
Disguise, I see, thou art a wickedness,
Wherein the pregnant enemy does much.
How easy is it for the proper-false
In women's waxen hearts to set their forms!
30   Alas, our frailty is the cause, not we,
For such as we are made of, such we be.
How will this fadge? My master loves her dearly,
And I, poor monster, fond as much on him,
And she, mistaken, seems to dote on me.
35   What will become of this? As I am man,
My state is desperate for my master's love.
As I am woman — now alas the day! —
What thriftless sighs shall poor Olivia breathe?
O time, thou must untangle this, not I.
40   It is too hard a knot for me t'untie.   *[Exit]*

---

12 peevishly willfully, foolishly   **13 so** in the same manner, i.e. thrown   **14 eye** plain sight
17 outside appearance   **18 made . . . of** had a good look at   **19 lost** made her lose
20 starts bursts   **distractedly** with agitation/madly   **22 in** by way of   **churlish** blunt,
ungracious   **25 were better** would be better off   **27 pregnant** resourceful   **enemy** probably
Satan   **28 proper-false** attractive but deceitful (men)   **29 set their forms** make their
impressions (like seals in wax)   **30 our . . . be** i.e. because women are made of frail material,
we are weak   **32 fadge** turn out   **33 monster** unnatural creature (being both man and
woman)   **fond** dote   **36 state . . . for** situation is hopeless with regard to   **38 thriftless**
unprofitable

Act 2 Scene 3

Enter Sir Toby and Sir Andrew

SIR TOBY   Approach, Sir Andrew. Not to be abed after midnight is to be up betimes, and *diluculo surgere*, thou know'st—

SIR ANDREW   Nay, by my troth I know not, but I know to be up
5   late is to be up late.

SIR TOBY   A false conclusion. I hate it as an unfilled can. To be up after midnight and to go to bed then is early: so that to go to bed after midnight is to go to bed betimes. Does not our lives consist of the four elements?

10   SIR ANDREW   Faith, so they say, but I think it rather consists of eating and drinking.

SIR TOBY   Thou'rt a scholar; let us therefore eat and drink. Marian, I say, a stoup of wine!

Enter Clown [Feste]

SIR ANDREW   Here comes the fool, i'faith.

15   FESTE   How now, my hearts! Did you never see the picture of 'we three'?

SIR TOBY   Welcome, ass. Now let's have a catch.

SIR ANDREW   By my troth the fool has an excellent breast. I had rather than forty shillings I had such a leg, and so sweet a
20   breath to sing, as the fool has. In sooth thou wast in very gracious fooling last night, when thou spokest of Pigrogromitus, of the Vapians passing the equinoctial of Queubus. 'Twas very good, i'faith. I sent thee sixpence for thy leman. Hadst it?

2.3   1 Approach come   **2 betimes** early   *diluculo surgere* (. . . *saluberrimum est*) "to get up early is most healthy" (Latin proverb)   **6 can** drinking vessel   **9 lives** i.e. living beings (Sir Andrew interprets as "way of life")   **four elements** earth, air, fire, and water, from which everything was thought to be made   **13 Marian** variant of Mary/Maria   **stoup** drinking vessel/measure of alcohol   **15 hearts** fine friends   **picture . . . three** captioned picture showing two fools or asses, so that the spectator is the third   **17 catch** musical round   **18 breast** set of lungs, singing voice   **19 leg** for dancing, or bowing before singing   **20 thou wast** you were   **22 Pigrogromitus . . . Queubus** words invented by Feste as examples of his feigned wisdom   **equinoctial** equator   **24 leman** sweetheart   **Hadst it?** Did you receive it?

25 FESTE   I did impeticos thy gratillity, for Malvolio's nose is no
                   whipstock. My lady has a white hand, and the Myrmidons
                   are no bottle-ale houses.

    SIR ANDREW   Excellent. Why, this is the best fooling, when all is
                   done. Now, a song.

30 SIR TOBY   Come on, there is sixpence for you. Let's   *Gives a coin*
                   have a song.   *to Feste*

    SIR ANDREW   There's a testril of me too. If one   *Gives another*
                   knight give a—   *coin*

    FESTE   Would you have a love song, or a song of good life?

35 SIR TOBY   A love song, a love song.

    SIR ANDREW   Ay, ay. I care not for good life.

    FESTE   O mistress mine, where are you roaming?   *Sings*
                   O stay and hear, your true love's coming,
                   That can sing both high and low.
40   Trip no further, pretty sweeting,
                   Journeys end in lovers meeting,
                   Every wise man's son doth know.

    SIR ANDREW   Excellent good, i'faith.

    SIR TOBY   Good, good.

45 FESTE   What is love? 'Tis not hereafter,   *Sings*
                   Present mirth hath present laughter.
                   What's to come is still unsure.
                   In delay there lies no plenty,
                   Then come kiss me, sweet and twenty,
50   Youth's a stuff will not endure.

    SIR ANDREW   A mellifluous voice, as I am true knight.

    SIR TOBY   A contagious breath.

    SIR ANDREW   Very sweet and contagious, i'faith.

---

25 impeticos i.e. pocket up   **gratillity** gratuity (another invented word)   **26 whipstock** whip-
handle   **Myrmidons** Achilles' followers; possible play on "Mermaid Inn," a tavern in
Shakespeare's London   **27 bottle-ale houses** low-class taverns   **32 testril** of sixpenny coin
from   **34 song . . . life** drinking song (Sir Andrew interprets **good** as "virtuous, moral")
39 high and low i.e. in terms of pitch or volume   **40 Trip** go, skip   **sweeting** darling
45 hereafter in the future   **47 still** always   **48 plenty** profit   **49 and twenty** an intensifier
(the singer's lover is "twenty times sweet")   **50 stuff** quality/material   **51 true** honest/
legitimate   **52 contagious breath** infectious breath/catchy song

SIR TOBY   To hear by the nose, it is dulcet in contagion. But
55   shall we make the welkin dance indeed? Shall we rouse the
        night owl in a catch that will draw three souls out of one
        weaver? Shall we do that?

SIR ANDREW   An you love me, let's do't. I am dog at a catch.

FESTE   By'r lady, sir, and some dogs will catch well.

60   SIR ANDREW   Most certain. Let our catch be, 'Thou knave'.

FESTE   'Hold thy peace, thou knave', knight? I shall be
        constrained in't to call thee knave, knight.

SIR ANDREW   'Tis not the first time I have constrained one to call
        me knave. Begin, fool: it begins 'Hold thy peace'.

65   FESTE   I shall never begin if I hold my peace.

SIR ANDREW   Good, i'faith. Come, begin.   *Catch sung*
        Enter Maria

MARIA   What a caterwauling do you keep here? If my lady
        have not called up her steward Malvolio and bid him turn
        you out of doors, never trust me.

70   SIR TOBY   My lady's a Catayan, we are politicians, Malvolio's a
        Peg-a-Ramsey, and 'Three merry men be we'. Am not I
        consanguineous? Am I not of her blood? Tillyvally. Lady!

        'There dwelt a man in Babylon, lady, lady!'   *Sings*

FESTE   Beshrew me, the knight's in admirable fooling.

75   SIR ANDREW   Ay, he does well enough if he be disposed, and so do
        I too: he does it with a better grace, but I do it more natural.

SIR TOBY   'O, the twelfth day of December'—   *Sings*

MARIA   For the love o'God, peace!

---

54 hear . . . nose i.e. if we inhaled sound   **dulcet in contagion** sweetly contagious
55 welkin sky   **rouse** startle/wake   **56 three souls** three singers would have thrice the effect;
powerful music was supposed to draw forth the soul   **57 weaver** often associated with psalm-
singing, so to excite one with a drinking song would be a real achievement   **58 dog** i.e. good
(Feste plays on the literal sense)   **59 By'r lady** by Our Lady, the Virgin Mary   **60 'Thou
knave'** the words of the round   **61 Hold thy peace** be quiet (subsequent dialogue plays on
"piece," penis)   **62 constrained** compelled   **67 keep** make   **68 steward** manager of
household affairs   **70 Catayan** Catharan (puritan)   **politicians** schemers   **71 Peg-a-
Ramsey** spying wife in a popular ballad   **'Three . . . we'** popular refrain from a song
72 consanguineous blood-related   **Tillyvally** nonsense   **73 'There . . . lady!'** the opening
and refrain of a song about the biblical tale of Susanna and the Elders   **74 Beshrew** curse
76 grace charm   **natural** convincingly/idiotically   **77 'O . . . December'** from an
unidentified song, possibly an erroneous reference to the twelfth day of Christmas (i.e. Twelfth
Night)

Enter Malvolio

MALVOLIO   My masters, are you mad? Or what are you? Have
80   you no wit, manners, nor honesty, but to gabble like tinkers
at this time of night? Do ye make an alehouse of my lady's
house, that ye squeak out your coziers' catches without any
mitigation or remorse of voice? Is there no respect of place,
persons, nor time in you?

85   SIR TOBY   We did keep time, sir, in our catches. Sneck up!

MALVOLIO   Sir Toby, I must be round with you. My lady bade me
tell you that though she harbours you as her kinsman, she's
nothing allied to your disorders. If you can separate yourself
and your misdemeanours, you are welcome to the house. If
90   not, an it would please you to take leave of her, she is very
willing to bid you farewell.

SIR TOBY   'Farewell, dear heart, since I must needs be   *Sings*
gone.'

MARIA   Nay, good Sir Toby.

FESTE   'His eyes do show his days are almost done.'   *Sings*

95   MALVOLIO   Is't even so?

SIR TOBY   'But I will never die.'   *Sings*

FESTE   Sir Toby, there you lie.

MALVOLIO   This is much credit to you.

SIR TOBY   'Shall I bid him go?'   *Sings*

100   FESTE   'What an if you do?'   *Sings*

SIR TOBY   'Shall I bid him go, and spare not?'   *Sings*

FESTE   'O no, no, no, no, you dare not.'   *Sings*

SIR TOBY   Out o'tune, sir, ye lie. Art any more than a steward?
Dost thou think, because thou art virtuous, there shall be no
105   more cakes and ale?

---

80 **wit** good sense   **honesty** decorum   **tinkers** popularly viewed as drunkards   **82 squeak
out** i.e. sing shrilly   **coziers'** cobblers'   **83 mitigation or remorse** considerate lowering
85 Sneck up! Shut up!/Buzz off!   **86 round** blunt   **87 harbours** lodges   **88 nothing allied**
not related to   **92 'Farewell . . . gone'** over the next few lines Sir Toby and Feste adapt lines
from a contemporary ballad   **95 Is't even so?** Is that the way things are?   **100 an if** if
101 spare not spare him not/be merciless   **103 Out o' tune** false   **Art** are (you)   **105 cakes
and ale** i.e. festivity, particularly abhorrent to one with puritan tendencies

FESTE   Yes, by Saint Anne, and ginger shall be hot i'th'mouth too.

SIR TOBY   Thou'rt i'th'right. Go, sir, rub your chain with crumbs. A stoup of wine, Maria!

110 MALVOLIO   Mistress Mary, if you prized my lady's favour at anything more than contempt, you would not give means for this uncivil rule; she shall know of it, by this hand.   *Exit*

MARIA   Go shake your ears.

SIR ANDREW   'Twere as good a deed as to drink when a man's
115   a-hungry, to challenge him the field, and then to break promise with him and make a fool of him.

SIR TOBY   Do't, knight. I'll write thee a challenge, or I'll deliver thy indignation to him by word of mouth.

MARIA   Sweet Sir Toby, be patient for tonight. Since the
120   youth of the count's was today with my lady, she is much out of quiet. For Monsieur Malvolio, let me alone with him: if I do not gull him into a nayword and make him a common recreation, do not think I have wit enough to lie straight in my bed. I know I can do it.

125 SIR TOBY   Possess us, possess us, tell us something of him.

MARIA   Marry, sir, sometimes he is a kind of puritan.

SIR ANDREW   O, if I thought that, I'd beat him like a dog!

SIR TOBY   What, for being a puritan? Thy exquisite reason, dear knight?

130 SIR ANDREW   I have no exquisite reason for't, but I have reason good enough.

---

106 **Saint Anne** mother of the Virgin Mary; another anti-puritan dig   **ginger** spice in ale/aphrodisiac   108 **rub . . . crumbs** polish your chain of office (reminding Malvolio of his servant status)   110 **prized** valued   111 **contempt** disrespect/disobedience   **give means** i.e. provide drink   112 **rule** behavior   113 **Go . . . ears** i.e. like an ass; a dismissive insult   115 **a-hungry** (very) hungry   **the field** to a duel   120 **out of quiet** agitated   121 **For** as for   **let . . . him** leave him to me   122 **gull** trick   **nayword** byword (for stupidity)   123 **recreation** source of amusement   125 **Possess** inform   126 **puritan** overly strict moralist; not necessarily a member of the extreme Protestant religious movement   128 **exquisite** ingenious/excellent

MARIA   The devil a puritan that he is, or anything
constantly, but a time-pleaser, an affectioned ass, that cons
state without book and utters it by great swarths. The best
135   persuaded of himself, so crammed, as he thinks, with
excellencies, that it is his grounds of faith that all that look
on him love him. And on that vice in him will my revenge
find notable cause to work.

SIR TOBY   What wilt thou do?

140   MARIA   I will drop in his way some obscure epistles of love,
wherein, by the colour of his beard, the shape of his leg, the
manner of his gait, the expressure of his eye, forehead, and
complexion, he shall find himself most feelingly personated.
I can write very like my lady your niece: on a forgotten
145   matter we can hardly make distinction of our hands.

SIR TOBY   Excellent! I smell a device.

SIR ANDREW   I have't in my nose too.

SIR TOBY   He shall think, by the letters that thou wilt drop,
that they come from my niece and that she's in love with
150   him.

MARIA   My purpose is, indeed, a horse of that colour.

SIR ANDREW   And your horse now would make him an ass.

MARIA   Ass, I doubt not.

SIR ANDREW   O, 'twill be admirable!

155   MARIA   Sport royal, I warrant you. I know my physic will
work with him. I will plant you two, and let the fool make a
third, where he shall find the letter. Observe his construction
of it. For this night, to bed, and dream on the event. Farewell.

Exit

---

133 **constantly** consistently   **time-pleaser** time-server, flatterer   **affectioned** pretentious
cons . . . book learns high-flown expressions by heart   134 **by great swarths** in broad
sweeps (like quantities of scythed hay)   **The best persuaded** having the highest opinion
136 **excellencies** excellent features/accomplishments   **grounds of faith** foundations of belief
140 **obscure epistles** ambiguous letters   142 **expressure** expression   143 **complexion**
appearance/coloring/temperament   **feelingly personated** accurately represented
144 **on . . . matter** when we have forgotten the circumstances in which something was written
or what it was about   145 **make distinction of** distinguish between   **hands** handwriting
146 **device** plot   153 **Ass** puns on "as"   155 **physic** medicine/treatment   157 **construction**
interpretation   158 **event** outcome

| | SIR TOBY | Good night, Penthesilea. |

160   SIR ANDREW   Before me, she's a good wench.

SIR TOBY   She's a beagle, true-bred, and one that adores me. What o'that?

SIR ANDREW   I was adored once too.

SIR TOBY   Let's to bed, knight. Thou hadst need send for more

165   money.

SIR ANDREW   If I cannot recover your niece, I am a foul way out.

SIR TOBY   Send for money, knight. If thou hast her not i'th'end, call me cut.

SIR ANDREW   If I do not, never trust me, take it how you will.

170   SIR TOBY   Come, come, I'll go burn some sack. 'Tis too late to go to bed now. Come, knight, come, knight.

Exeunt

Act 2 Scene 4

Enter Duke [Orsino], Viola, Curio and others

ORSINO   Give me some music.— Now, good morrow, friends.
Now, good Cesario, but that piece of song,
That old and antique song we heard last night;
Methought it did relieve my passion much,

5   More than light airs and recollected terms
Of these most brisk and giddy-pacèd times.
Come, but one verse.

CURIO   He is not here, so please your lordship, that should sing it.

10   ORSINO   Who was it?

CURIO   Feste, the jester, my lord; a fool that the lady Olivia's father took much delight in. He is about the house.

---

159 Penthesilea Queen of the Amazons; probably refers to Maria's shortness   **160 Before me** mild oath like "upon my soul"   **161 beagle** skillful hunting dog   **166 recover** obtain/win **foul way out** miserably far from success/badly out of pocket   **168 cut** cart-horse (castrated or with docked tail)/vagina   **170 burn** warm/sweeten with burnt sugar   **sack** Spanish white wine   **2.4**   **2 but** (I want to hear) only   **3 antique** quaint/old   **4 passion** suffering   **5 airs** melodies   **recollected terms** studied, artificial expressions

ORSINO   Seek him out, and play the tune the while.

[*Exit Curio*]

Come hither, boy. If ever thou shalt love,   *Music plays*

15   In the sweet pangs of it remember me,

For such as I am, all true lovers are:

Unstaid and skittish in all motions else,

Save in the constant image of the creature

That is beloved. How dost thou like this tune?

20   VIOLA   It gives a very echo to the seat

Where love is throned.

ORSINO   Thou dost speak masterly.

My life upon't, young though thou art, thine eye

Hath stayed upon some favour that it loves:

25   Hath it not, boy?

VIOLA   A little, by your favour.

ORSINO   What kind of woman is't?

VIOLA   Of your complexion.

ORSINO   She is not worth thee, then. What years, i'faith?

30   VIOLA   About your years, my lord.

ORSINO   Too old by heaven. Let still the woman take

An elder than herself, so wears she to him,

So sways she level in her husband's heart.

For, boy, however we do praise ourselves,

35   Our fancies are more giddy and unfirm,

More longing, wavering, sooner lost and worn,

Than women's are.

VIOLA   I think it well, my lord.

ORSINO   Then let thy love be younger than thyself,

40   Or thy affection cannot hold the bent,

---

13 **the while** in the meantime   17 **Unstaid and skittish** unsettled and fickle   **motions else**
other emotions   18 **constant** faithful (contemplation of the)   20 **gives . . . throned** reflects
the heart exactly   22 **masterly** from experience/knowingly   24 **stayed** lingered   **favour**
face   26 **by your favour** if you please (plays on the sense of "on your face")   31 **still** always
32 **wears she** she adapts herself   33 **sways she level** swings in perfect balance/exerts
constant influence   35 **fancies** infatuations   36 **worn** exhausted   38 **I . . . well** I believe it
40 **hold the bent** hold steady (from archery: holding the bow taut)

For women are as roses, whose fair flower
Being once displayed, doth fall that very hour.

VIOLA   And so they are. Alas, that they are so.
To die, even when they to perfection grow!

Enter Curio and Clown [Feste]

45 ORSINO   O, fellow, come, the song we had last   *To Feste*
 night.—
Mark it, Cesario, it is old and plain;
The spinsters and the knitters in the sun
And the free maids that weave their thread with bones
Do use to chant it. It is silly sooth,
50 And dallies with the innocence of love,
Like the old age.

FESTE   Are you ready, sir?

ORSINO   I prithee sing.   *Music*

FESTE   *The song*

Come away, come away, death,   *Sings*
55 And in sad cypress let me be laid.
Fly away, fly away, breath,
I am slain by a fair cruel maid.
My shroud of white, stuck all with yew,
O, prepare it!
60 My part of death, no one so true
Did share it.

Not a flower, not a flower, sweet
On my black coffin let there be strewn.
Not a friend, not a friend greet
65 My poor corpse, where my bones shall be thrown.
A thousand thousand sighs to save,

---

42 displayed unfurled, in full bloom   **47 Mark** take note of   **48 spinsters** spinners
49 free carefree/innocent   **weave . . . bones** make lace with bone bobbins   **49 Do use** are
accustomed   **silly sooth** simple truth   **50 dallies** deals lightly/toys   **51 old age** bygone
times, good old days   **54 away** here   **55 cypress** cypress-wood coffin/among sprigs of
cypress (associated with mourning)   **58 stuck** adorned, strewn   **yew** yew twigs, also
emblematic of mourning   **60 My . . . it** I am the truest lover who ever died for love
63 strewn pronounced "strown"

                    Lay me, O, where
                    Sad true lover never find my grave,
                    To weep there!

70 ORSINO   There's for thy pains.

    FESTE   No pains, sir. I take pleasure in singing, sir.

    ORSINO   I'll pay thy pleasure then.

    FESTE   Truly, sir, and pleasure will be paid, one time or
                another.

75 ORSINO   Give me now leave to leave thee.

    FESTE   Now, the melancholy god protect thee, and the
                tailor make thy doublet of changeable taffeta, for thy mind is
                a very opal. I would have men of such constancy put to sea,
                that their business might be everything and their intent
80   everywhere, for that's it that always makes a good voyage of
                nothing. Farewell.   *Exit*

    ORSINO   Let all the rest give place.   *Curio and Attendants stand aside*
                                                 Once more, Cesario,
                Get thee to yond same sovereign cruelty:
                Tell her my love, more noble than the world,
85   Prizes not quantity of dirty lands.
                The parts that fortune hath bestowed upon her
                Tell her, I hold as giddily as fortune.
                But 'tis that miracle and queen of gems
                That nature pranks her in attracts my soul.

90 VIOLA   But if she cannot love you, sir?

    ORSINO   I cannot be so answered.

    VIOLA   Sooth, but you must.
                Say that some lady, as perhaps there is,
                Hath for your love as great a pang of heart

---

73 **pleasure . . . paid** with pain (proverbial)   75 **leave to leave** permission to dismiss
76 **melancholy god** Saturn, thought to govern melancholy dispositions   77 **doublet** close-
fitting jacket   **changeable taffeta** shot silk, the color of which changes depending on the light
78 **opal** iridescent gem of changeable color   **men . . . constancy** i.e. inconstant men
79 **their . . . everywhere** "he that is everywhere is nowhere" (proverbial)   80 **that's . . .
nothing** that's the attitude that considers a useless voyage to be profitable   82 **give place**
leave   85 **dirty** dishonorably acquired/despicable/muddy   86 **parts** attributes, i.e. wealth
87 **giddily** lightly   **fortune** traditionally held to be fickle   88 **miracle . . . gems** i.e. Olivia's
beauty   89 **pranks** adorns

95 As you have for Olivia: you cannot love her.
You tell her so. Must she not then be answered?

ORSINO   There is no woman's sides
Can bide the beating of so strong a passion
As love doth give my heart, no woman's heart
100 So big, to hold so much. They lack retention.
Alas, their love may be called appetite,
No motion of the liver, but the palate,
That suffer surfeit, cloyment and revolt.
But mine is all as hungry as the sea,
105 And can digest as much. Make no compare
Between that love a woman can bear me
And that I owe Olivia.

VIOLA   Ay, but I know—

ORSINO   What dost thou know?

110 VIOLA   Too well what love women to men may owe:
In faith, they are as true of heart as we.
My father had a daughter loved a man,
As it might be, perhaps, were I a woman,
I should your lordship.

115 ORSINO   And what's her history?

VIOLA   A blank, my lord. She never told her love,
But let concealment, like a worm i'th'bud,
Feed on her damask cheek: she pined in thought,
And with a green and yellow melancholy
120 She sat like patience on a monument,
Smiling at grief. Was not this love indeed?
We men may say more, swear more, but indeed
Our shows are more than will, for still we prove
Much in our vows, but little in our love.

---

96 be answered satisfied   **98 bide** withstand   **100 retention** the power to retain (emotion)
101 appetite desire/fancy   **102 motion** impulse/emotion   **liver** thought to be the seat of
strong passion   **palate** organ of taste, i.e. easily satisfied   **103 suffer** undergo   **surfeit**
sickening overindulgence   **cloyment** excessive gratification   **revolt** revulsion (of appetite)
104 mine i.e. my love   **105 compare** comparison   **107 owe** have for   **115 history** story
118 damask pink, like the damask rose   **119 green and yellow** sickly, pale and sallow
120 patience . . . monument carved figure on a memorial   **123 shows** outward displays
are more have more substance   **will** our desires   **still** always

125	ORSINO	But died thy sister of her love, my boy?

ORSINO But died thy sister of her love, my boy?

VIOLA I am all the daughters of my father's house,
And all the brothers too, and yet I know not.
Sir, shall I to this lady?

ORSINO Ay, that's the theme.

130 To her in haste: give her this jewel: say   *Gives a jewel*
My love can give no place, bide no denay.   *Exeunt*

Act 2 Scene 5   *running scene 10*

Enter Sir Toby, Sir Andrew and Fabian

SIR TOBY Come thy ways, Signior Fabian.

FABIAN Nay, I'll come. If I lose a scruple of this sport, let me
be boiled to death with melancholy.

SIR TOBY Wouldst thou not be glad to have the niggardly
5 rascally sheep-biter come by some notable shame?

FABIAN I would exult, man. You know he brought me out
o'favour with my lady about a bear-baiting here.

SIR TOBY To anger him we'll have the bear again, and we will
fool him black and blue. Shall we not, Sir Andrew?

10 SIR ANDREW An we do not, it is pity of our lives.

Enter Maria

SIR TOBY Here comes the little villain.— How now,   *To Maria*
my metal of India?

MARIA Get ye all three into the box-tree: Malvolio's coming
down this walk. He has been yonder i'the sun practising
15 behaviour to his own shadow this half hour. Observe him,
for the love of mockery, for I know this letter will make a
contemplative idiot of him. Close, in the name of   *They hide*

---

128 to go to   **131 give no place** not give way   **denay** denial   **2.5   1 Come thy ways** come
along   **2 scruple** tiny amount   **3 boiled** puns on (black) "bile," the cause of **melancholy**;
also a joke, since **melancholy** was a cold, dry humor   **4 niggardly** mean-minded   **5 sheep-
biter** nasty, shifty fellow (literally, a dog that attacks sheep)   **7 bear-baiting** a pastime that was
particularly disapproved of by puritans   **9 fool . . . blue** bruise him (metaphorically) with
fooling   **10 pity . . . lives** a pity we should live   **12 metal of India** i.e. pure gold, treasure
13 box-tree thick evergreen shrub used in ornamental gardens   **14 walk** path   **15 behaviour**
courtly gestures   **17 contemplative** preoccupied/mindlessly gazing   **Close** stay hidden

jesting! Lie thou there, for here comes the trout that must be caught with tickling.   *Puts a letter on the ground*

Exit

Enter Malvolio   ↓*Sir Toby and the others are not heard by Malvolio*↓

20 MALVOLIO   'Tis but fortune, all is fortune. Maria once told me she did affect me, and I have heard herself come thus near, that should she fancy, it should be one of my complexion. Besides, she uses me with a more exalted respect than anyone else that follows her. What should I think on't?

25 SIR TOBY   Here's an overweening rogue!

    FABIAN   O, peace! Contemplation makes a rare turkey-cock of him. How he jets under his advanced plumes!

    SIR ANDREW   'Slight, I could so beat the rogue!

    SIR TOBY   Peace, I say.

30 MALVOLIO   To be Count Malvolio!

    SIR TOBY   Ah, rogue!

    SIR ANDREW   Pistol him, pistol him.

    SIR TOBY   Peace, peace!

    MALVOLIO   There is example for't: the lady of the Strachy
35   married the yeoman of the wardrobe.

    SIR ANDREW   Fie on him, Jezebel!

    FABIAN   O, peace! Now he's deeply in: look how imagination blows him.

    MALVOLIO   Having been three months married to her, sitting in
40   my state—

    SIR TOBY   O, for a stone-bow to hit him in the eye!

---

19 tickling i.e. flattery; one method of catching **trout** is to stroke them under their gills
21 she Olivia   **affect** love/feel fondness for   **thus near** i.e. close to saying   **22 fancy** love
23 uses treats   **24 follows** serves   **25 overweening** arrogant/overambitious   **26 rare**
splendid   **turkey-cock** a proverbially proud, vain bird   **27 jets** struts   **advanced plumes**
raised feathers   **28 'Slight** (by) God's light   **32 Pistol** shoot   **34 example** precedent
lady . . . wardrobe unknown allusion to the marriage of a woman to her social inferior
35 yeoman . . . wardrobe servant in charge of household clothes and linen   **36 Jezebel** in
the Bible, proud wife of Ahab, King of Israel; term for a wicked, deceptive, or lascivious woman
37 in absorbed in his own fantasies   **38 blows him** puffs him up   **40 state** canopied chair of
state   **41 stone-bow** crossbow that shoots stones

	MALVOLIO	Calling my officers about me, in my branched velvet gown, having come from a daybed, where I have left Olivia sleeping—
45	SIR TOBY	Fire and brimstone!
	FABIAN	O, peace, peace!
	MALVOLIO	And then to have the humour of state, and after a demure travel of regard, telling them I know my place as I would they should do theirs, to ask for my kinsman Toby—
50	SIR TOBY	Bolts and shackles!
	FABIAN	O peace, peace, peace! Now, now.
	MALVOLIO	Seven of my people, with an obedient start, make out for him. I frown the while, and perchance wind up my watch, or play with my— some rich jewel. Toby approaches;
55		curtsies there to me—
	SIR TOBY	Shall this fellow live?
	FABIAN	Though our silence be drawn from us with cars, yet peace.
	MALVOLIO	I extend my hand to him thus, quenching my
60		familiar smile with an austere regard of control—
	SIR TOBY	And does not Toby take you a blow o'the lips then?
	MALVOLIO	Saying, 'Cousin Toby, my fortunes having cast me on your niece give me this prerogative of speech'—
	SIR TOBY	What, what?
65	MALVOLIO	'You must amend your drunkenness.'
	SIR TOBY	Out, scab!
	FABIAN	Nay, patience, or we break the sinews of our plot.
	MALVOLIO	'Besides, you waste the treasure of your time with a foolish knight'—

---

42 officers household servants   **branched** embroidered with a branched pattern or with images of foliage   **43 daybed** sofa/bed for daytime reclining (with sexual associations) **47 humour of state** temperament/power of one in authority   **48 demure . . . regard** solemn survey of the room and company   **49 would** wish   **Toby** Malvolio omits "Sir"   **50 Bolts and shackles!** restraints for a prisoner   **52 people** servants   **start** sudden movement   **make out** go   **53 perchance** perhaps   **54 my—** perhaps chain of office, which Malvolio momentarily forgets he would not be wearing, but he could be referring to anything; a genital quibble is probably present   **55 curtsies** bows   **57 cars** chariots/carts, i.e. by torture   **60 familiar** friendly   **regard of control** authoritative look   **61 take** strike, give   **62 Cousin** kinsman **63 prerogative** due privilege, right   **66 scab** scoundrel   **67 sinews** muscles, strength

70	SIR ANDREW	That's me, I warrant you.
	MALVOLIO	'One Sir Andrew'—
	SIR ANDREW	I knew 'twas I, for many do call me fool.
	MALVOLIO	What employment have we here? *Picks up the letter*
	FABIAN	Now is the woodcock near the gin.
75	SIR TOBY	O, peace! And the spirit of humours intimate reading aloud to him.
	MALVOLIO	By my life, this is my lady's hand these be her very C's, her U's and her T's, and thus makes she her great P's. It is in contempt of question her hand.
80	SIR ANDREW	Her C's, her U's and her T's. Why that?
	MALVOLIO	'To the unknown beloved, this, and my good *Reads* wishes.' Her very phrases! By your leave, wax. Soft! And the impressure her Lucrece, with which she uses to seal. 'Tis my lady. To whom should this be?
85	FABIAN	This wins him, liver and all.
	MALVOLIO	'Jove knows I love, *Reads*
		But who?
		Lips, do not move.
		No man must know.'
90		'No man must know.' What follows? The numbers altered! 'No man must know.' If this should be thee, Malvolio?
	SIR TOBY	Marry, hang thee, brock!
	MALVOLIO	'I may command where I adore, *Reads*
		But silence, like a Lucrece knife,
95		With bloodless stroke my heart doth gore:
		M.O.A.I. doth sway my life.'
	FABIAN	A fustian riddle!
	SIR TOBY	Excellent wench, say I.

---

73 employment business   **74 woodcock** proverbially stupid bird   **gin** trap   **75 humours** whims, moods   **intimate** suggest   **77 hand** handwriting   **78 C's . . . T's** "cut" was slang for "vagina," but the joke may well be on "cunt" (with **and** as "n")   **great P's** uppercase P's/noble vagina ("piece")/copious urination   **79 in contempt of** beyond   **83 impressure** imprint, seal   **Lucrece** Olivia's seal-ring bears the image of Lucrece, Roman heroine who committed suicide after being raped   **uses to seal** customarily seals   **85 liver** seat of passion **90 numbers altered** meter changed   **92 brock** badger, used contemptuously   **94 Lucrece knife** knife Lucrece used to kill herself   **96 sway** rule   **97 fustian** nonsensical/pompous (literally, inferior cloth)

MALVOLIO   'M.O.A.I. doth sway my life.' Nay, but first let me see,
100   let me see, let me see.

FABIAN   What dish o'poison has she dressed him.

SIR TOBY   And with what wing the staniel checks at it!

MALVOLIO   'I may command where I adore.' Why, she may
command me! I serve her, she is my lady. Why, this is evident to
105   any formal capacity. There is no obstruction in this. And the
end — what should that alphabetical position portend? If I
could make that resemble something in me. Softly: M.O.A.I.—

SIR TOBY   O, ay, make up that. He is now at a cold scent.

FABIAN   Sowter will cry upon't for all this, though it be as
110   rank as a fox.

MALVOLIO   M. — Malvolio. M. — Why, that begins my name!

FABIAN   Did not I say he would work it out? The cur is
excellent at faults.

MALVOLIO   M. — But then there is no consonancy in the sequel
115   that suffers under probation: 'A' should follow but 'O' does.

FABIAN   And O shall end, I hope.

SIR TOBY   Ay, or I'll cudgel him, and make him cry O!

MALVOLIO   And then I comes behind.

FABIAN   Ay, an you had any eye behind you, you might see
120   more detraction at your heels than fortunes before you.

MALVOLIO   M.O.A.I. This simulation is not as the former. And
yet, to crush this a little, it would bow to me, for every one of
these letters are in my name. Soft, here follows prose: 'If this
fall into thy hand, revolve. In my stars I am above   *Reads*
125   thee, but be not afraid of greatness: some are born great,

---

101 What what a   **dressed** prepared for   **102 wing** flight/speed   **staniel** kestrel, or small
falcon   **checks** swoops   **105 formal capacity** normal intelligence   **obstruction** obstacle
106 position arrangement   **portend** mean   **108 O, ay** puns on the O . . . I of M.O.A.I.
make up work out   **at . . . scent** has lost the trail   **109 Sowter** name of a hound (a "souter"
was a cobbler)   **cry** bark   **110 rank** foul-smelling   **112 cur** dog   **113 faults** finding the
scent again after the trail has gone cold   **114 consonancy . . . sequel** consistency of pattern
115 suffers holds up   **probation** investigation   **116 O shall end** O ends Malvolio's name/a
cry of misery will end this business/the hangman's noose ends life   **119 eye** puns on **Ay** and **I**
120 detraction defamation, slander   **121 simulation** disguised meaning   **former** earlier,
clearer parts of the letter   **122 crush** force a meaning from   **bow** yield   **124 revolve**
consider (with play on "turn round," which may cue Malvolio to do so)   **stars** fortunes

some achieve greatness, and some have greatness thrust
upon 'em. Thy Fates open their hands. Let thy blood and spirit
embrace them. And to inure thyself to what thou art like to
be, cast thy humble slough and appear fresh. Be opposite with
a kinsman, surly with servants. Let thy tongue tang
arguments of state; put thyself into the trick of singularity.
She thus advises thee that sighs for thee. Remember who
commended thy yellow stockings, and wished to see thee ever
cross-gartered. I say, remember. Go to, thou art made, if thou
desirest to be so. If not, let me see thee a steward still, the
fellow of servants, and not worthy to touch Fortune's fingers.
Farewell. She that would alter services with thee,

                    The Fortunate-Unhappy.'

Daylight and champaign discovers not more. This is open. I
will be proud, I will read politic authors, I will baffle Sir
Toby, I will wash off gross acquaintance, I will be point-
device the very man. I do not now fool myself, to let
imagination jade me; for every reason excites to this, that
my lady loves me. She did commend my yellow stockings of
late, she did praise my leg being cross-gartered. And in this
she manifests herself to my love, and with a kind of
injunction drives me to these habits of her liking. I thank
my stars, I am happy. I will be strange, stout, in yellow
stockings, and cross-gartered, even with the swiftness of
putting on. Jove and my stars be praised! Here is yet a
postscript: 'Thou canst not choose but know   *Reads*
who I am. If thou entertainest my love, let it appear in thy
smiling. Thy smiles become thee well: therefore in my

130
135
140
145
150

127 **open their hands** offer bounty   **blood and spirit** i.e. all of you, body and soul
128 **embrace** willingly accept   **inure** accustom   **like** likely   129 **cast** cast off   **slough** outer
skin   **opposite** antagonistic/contradictory   130 **tang . . . state** ring out on political topics
131 **trick of singularity** peculiar, distinctive behavior   133 **ever** at all times   134 **cross-
gartered** wearing garters crossed near the knee   **Go to** i.e. come on   137 **alter services**
exchange places of mistress and servant; with sexual innuendo   138 **Fortunate-Unhappy**
i.e. wealthy, but lacking requited love   139 **champaign** open countryside   **discovers** reveals
open clear   140 **politic** political/prudent   **baffle** publicly disgrace   141 **gross** dull/base
point-device to the last detail   143 **jade** deceive   **excites** urges   146 **manifests herself to**
reveals herself as   147 **injunction** order   **habits** ways of dressing/behavior   148 **happy**
fortunate   **strange** aloof   **stout** proud, haughty   152 **entertainest** welcome, accept

presence still smile, dear my sweet, I prithee.' Jove, I thank
155   thee. I will smile. I will do everything that thou wilt have
me.   *Exit*

Sir Toby, Sir Andrew and Fabian come out of hiding

FABIAN   I will not give my part of this sport for a pension of
thousands to be paid from the Sophy.

SIR TOBY   I could marry this wench for this device.

160   SIR ANDREW   So could I too.

SIR TOBY   And ask no other dowry with her but such another
jest.

Enter Maria

SIR ANDREW   Nor I neither.

FABIAN   Here comes my noble gull-catcher.

165   SIR TOBY   Wilt thou set thy foot o'my neck?

SIR ANDREW   Or o'mine either?

SIR TOBY   Shall I play my freedom at tray-trip, and become thy
bondslave?

SIR ANDREW   I'faith, or I either?

170   SIR TOBY   Why, thou hast put him in such a dream that when
the image of it leaves him, he must run mad.

MARIA   Nay, but say true, does it work upon him?

SIR TOBY   Like aqua-vitae with a midwife.

MARIA   If you will then see the fruits of the sport, mark his
175   first approach before my lady: he will come to her in yellow
stockings, and 'tis a colour she abhors, and cross-gartered, a
fashion she detests. And he will smile upon her, which will
now be so unsuitable to her disposition, being addicted to a
melancholy as she is, that it cannot but turn him into a
180   notable contempt. If you will see it, follow me.

SIR TOBY   To the gates of Tartar, thou most excellent devil
of wit!

SIR ANDREW   I'll make one too.   *Exeunt*

---

154 **still** always   158 **Sophy** Shah of Persia   159 **device** plot   164 **gull-catcher** fool-
trapper/trickster   165 **Wilt . . . neck?** i.e. I submit totally to you   167 **play** gamble   **tray-trip**
type of dicing game   168 **bondslave** slave   173 **aqua-vitae** strong spirits, such as brandy
174 **fruits** outcome   180 **contempt** object of contempt   181 **Tartar** Tartarus, hell of classical
mythology   183 **make one** join in, tag along

Act 3 Scene 1

Enter Viola and Clown [Feste, with a tabor]

VIOLA   Save thee, friend, and thy music. Dost thou live by thy tabor?

FESTE   No, sir, I live by the church.

VIOLA   Art thou a churchman?

5 **FESTE**   No such matter, sir. I do live by the church, for I do live at my house, and my house doth stand by the church.

VIOLA   So thou mayst say, the king lies by a beggar, if a beggar dwell near him, or the church stands by thy tabor, if thy tabor stand by the church.

10 **FESTE**   You have said, sir. To see this age! A sentence is but a cheveril glove to a good wit. How quickly the wrong side may be turned outward!

VIOLA   Nay, that's certain. They that dally nicely with words may quickly make them wanton.

15 **FESTE**   I would, therefore, my sister had had no name, sir.

VIOLA   Why, man?

FESTE   Why, sir, her name's a word, and to dally with that word might make my sister wanton. But indeed, words are very rascals since bonds disgraced them.

20 **VIOLA**   Thy reason, man?

FESTE   Troth, sir, I can yield you none without words, and words are grown so false, I am loath to prove reason with them.

VIOLA   I warrant thou art a merry fellow and car'st for
25 nothing.

FESTE   Not so, sir, I do care for something. But in my conscience, sir, I do not care for you: if that be to care for nothing, sir, I would it would make you invisible.

3.1   *tabor* small drum   **1 Save** God save   **live by** earn your living with (Feste plays on the sense of **by** as "next to")   **7 lies by** dwells near/sleeps with   **8 stands** is maintained
9 stand is placed   **10 You have said** you have had your say/fair enough   **sentence** saying
11 cheveril kidskin (pliable leather)   **13 dally nicely** play subtly/triflingly   **14 wanton**
uncontrolled, ambiguous/lecherous   **19 bonds** legal contracts   **disgraced them** i.e. by
suggesting that a man's word alone was not enough   **21 yield** give

| | VIOLA | Art not thou the lady Olivia's fool? |

VIOLA   Art not thou the lady Olivia's fool?

30 FESTE   No, indeed, sir, the lady Olivia has no folly. She will keep no fool, sir, till she be married, and fools are as like husbands as pilchards are to herrings: the husband's the bigger. I am indeed not her fool, but her corrupter of words.

VIOLA   I saw thee late at the count Orsino's.

35 FESTE   Foolery, sir, does walk about the orb like the sun, it shines everywhere. I would be sorry, sir, but the fool should be as oft with your master as with my mistress. I think I saw your wisdom there.

VIOLA   Nay, an thou pass upon me, I'll no more with thee.
40 Hold, there's expenses for thee.   *Gives money*

FESTE   Now Jove, in his next commodity of hair, send thee a beard!

VIOLA   By my troth I'll tell thee, I am almost sick for one—
though I would not have it grow on my chin.— Is   *Aside*
45 thy lady within?

FESTE   Would not a pair of these have bred, sir?

VIOLA   Yes, being kept together and put to use.

FESTE   I would play Lord Pandarus of Phrygia, sir, to bring a Cressida to this Troilus.

50 VIOLA   I understand you, sir. 'Tis well   *Gives more money*
begged.

FESTE   The matter, I hope, is not great, sir; begging but a beggar. Cressida was a beggar. My lady is within, sir. I will conster to them whence you come. Who you are and what
55 you would are out of my welkin. I might say 'element', but the word is over-worn.   *Exit*

---

32 pilchards small fish that resemble herring   **34 late** recently   **35 orb** planet, world
36 but were it not for the fact that   **38 your wisdom** i.e. you, a hired servant/fool   **39 pass
upon** jest at/judge   **41 commodity** supply   **43 for one** wanting a beard/from love for a
bearded man   **46 these** i.e. coins   **bred** multiplied; Feste asks for more money   **47 put to
use** invested for profit (plays on the sense of "having had sex")   **48 Pandarus** uncle to
Cressida and go-between for his niece and her lover **Troilus   Phrygia** country in Asia Minor
where Troy was situated   **53 Cressida . . . beggar** in some versions of the story, Cressida
became a beggar with leprosy   **54 conster** explain   **55 out . . . welkin** beyond me   **welkin**
sky, heavens   **element** sphere of knowledge/sky

VIOLA   This fellow is wise enough to play the fool,
And to do that well craves a kind of wit:
He must observe their mood on whom he jests,
60 The quality of persons, and the time,
And, like the haggard, check at every feather
That comes before his eye. This is a practice
As full of labour as a wise man's art,
For folly that he wisely shows is fit;
65 But wise men, folly-fall'n, quite taint their wit.

Enter Sir Toby and Andrew

SIR TOBY   Save you, gentleman.

VIOLA   And you, sir.

SIR ANDREW   *Dieu vous garde, monsieur.*

VIOLA   *Et vous aussi. Votre serviteur.*

70 SIR ANDREW   I hope, sir, you are, and I am yours.

SIR TOBY   Will you encounter the house? My niece is desirous
you should enter, if your trade be to her.

VIOLA   I am bound to your niece, sir. I mean she is the list of
my voyage.

75 SIR TOBY   Taste your legs, sir, put them to motion.

VIOLA   My legs do better understand me, sir, than I
understand what you mean by bidding me taste my legs.

SIR TOBY   I mean, to go, sir, to enter.

VIOLA   I will answer you with gait and entrance. But we are
80 prevented.

Enter Olivia and Gentlewoman [Maria]

Most excellent accomplished lady, the heavens rain odours
on you!

SIR ANDREW   That youth's a rare courtier. 'Rain   *To Toby*
odours', well.

---

58 craves requires   **60 quality** character/rank   **61 haggard** untrained hawk   **check** swoop
62 practice occupation   **64 is fit** suits the purpose   **65 folly-fall'n** stooping to foolishness
68 *Dieu . . . monsieur* "God save you, sir" (French)   **69** *Et . . . serviteur* "And you, too. [I am]
your servant" (French)   **71 encounter** approach/enter   **72 trade** business, with sexual
innuendo   **to** with, concerning   **73 bound to** heading for   **list** limit, objective   **75 Taste**
try out   **76 understand** support/comprehend   **79 gait and entrance** corresponding nouns to
Sir Toby's verbs; **gait** puns on "gate"   **80 prevented** anticipated/forestalled   **81 the** may the
odours sweet smells

85   VIOLA   My matter hath no voice, lady, but to your own
most pregnant and vouchsafed ear.

SIR ANDREW   'Odours,' 'pregnant' and 'vouchsafed'.   *To Toby*
I'll get 'em all three all ready.

OLIVIA   Let the garden door be shut, and leave me to my
90   hearing.—

[*Exeunt Sir Toby, Sir Andrew and Maria*]
Give me your hand, sir.

VIOLA   My duty, madam, and most humble service.

OLIVIA   What is your name?

VIOLA   Cesario is your servant's name, fair princess.

95   OLIVIA   My servant, sir? 'Twas never merry world
Since lowly feigning was called compliment.
You're servant to the count Orsino, youth.

VIOLA   And he is yours, and his must needs be yours:
Your servant's servant is your servant, madam.

100   OLIVIA   For him, I think not on him: for his thoughts,
Would they were blanks, rather than filled with me!

VIOLA   Madam, I come to whet your gentle thoughts
On his behalf.

OLIVIA   O, by your leave, I pray you.
105   I bade you never speak again of him;
But, would you undertake another suit,
I had rather hear you to solicit that
Than music from the spheres.

VIOLA   Dear lady—

110   OLIVIA   Give me leave, beseech you. I did send,
After the last enchantment you did here,
A ring in chase of you: so did I abuse

---

85 **hath no voice** cannot be uttered   86 **pregnant** receptive   **vouchsafed** (kindly) bestowed,
i.e. attentive   88 **all ready** committed to memory, ready for use   90 **hearing** audience (with
Cesario)   95 **'Twas . . . world** proverbial: things haven't been the same   96 **lowly feigning**
pretended modesty.   **compliment** courtesy   98 **yours** your servant   **his** i.e. his servants
100 **For** as for   101 **blanks** blank paper/unstamped coins   106 **suit** petition, courtship
107 **solicit** urge   108 **music . . . spheres** planets and stars were thought to be surrounded by
hollow spheres that produced beautiful music as they rotated   110 **leave** permission (to
speak)   112 **abuse** wrong/disgrace

Myself, my servant and, I fear me, you.
Under your hard construction must I sit,
115 To force that on you, in a shameful cunning,
Which you knew none of yours. What might you think?
Have you not set mine honour at the stake
And baited it with all th'unmuzzled thoughts
That tyrannous heart can think? To one of your receiving
120 Enough is shown: a cypress, not a bosom,
Hides my heart. So, let me hear you speak.

VIOLA   I pity you.

OLIVIA   That's a degree to love.

VIOLA   No, not a grize, for 'tis a vulgar proof,
125 That very oft we pity enemies.

OLIVIA   Why, then, methinks 'tis time to smile again.
O, world, how apt the poor are to be proud!
If one should be a prey, how much the better
To fall before the lion than the wolf!   *Clock strikes*
130 The clock upbraids me with the waste of time.
Be not afraid, good youth, I will not have you:
And yet, when wit and youth is come to harvest,
Your wife is like to reap a proper man.
There lies your way, due west.

135 VIOLA   Then westward-ho! Grace and good disposition
Attend your ladyship!
You'll nothing, madam, to my lord by me?

OLIVIA   Stay.
I prithee tell me what thou think'st of me.

140 VIOLA   That you do think you are not what you are.

OLIVIA   If I think so, I think the same of you.

VIOLA   Then think you right: I am not what I am.

OLIVIA   I would you were as I would have you be.

---

114 **construction** judgment/interpretation (of my conduct)   115 **To force** for forcing
117 **stake** post to which a bear is chained for baiting by dogs   119 **receiving** understanding
120 **cypress** light transparent material   123 **degree** step   124 **grize** step   **vulgar proof**
common experience   126 **smile again** i.e. throw off melancholy   129 **lion** a more noble
adversary   133 **proper** handsome/worthy   135 **disposition** state of mind   137 **You'll** you'll
send   140 **what you are** i.e. in love with me (a woman/a servant)

VIOLA   Would it be better, madam, than I am?
145   I wish it might, for now I am your fool.

OLIVIA   O, what a deal of scorn looks beautiful
In the contempt and anger of his lip!
A murd'rous guilt shows not itself more soon
Than love that would seem hid: love's night is noon.
150   Cesario, by the roses of the spring,
By maidhood, honour, truth and everything,
I love thee so that, maugre all thy pride,
Nor wit nor reason can my passion hide.
Do not extort thy reasons from this clause,
155   For that I woo, thou therefore hast no cause,
But rather reason thus with reason fetter:
Love sought is good, but given unsought is better.

VIOLA   By innocence I swear, and by my youth,
I have one heart, one bosom and one truth,
160   And that no woman has, nor never none
Shall mistress be of it, save I alone.
And so adieu, good madam. Never more
Will I my master's tears to you deplore.

OLIVIA   Yet come again, for thou perhaps mayst move
165   That heart which now abhors, to like his love.   *Exeunt*

Act 3 Scene 2
running scene 11

Enter Sir Toby, Sir Andrew and Fabian

SIR ANDREW   No, faith, I'll not stay a jot longer.

SIR TOBY   Thy reason, dear venom, give thy reason.

FABIAN   You must needs yield your reason, Sir Andrew.

---

145 I . . . fool you make me look foolish   **146 deal** quantity   **149 love's . . . noon** i.e. despite trying to conceal itself, love is obvious   **151 maidhood** virginity   **152 maugre** in spite of **153 Nor** neither   **154 extort . . . clause** extract reason from this premise   **155 For that** because   **no cause** need to woo in return   **156 reason . . . fetter** restrain your reason with the following reasoning   **163 deplore** lament, recount sorrowfully   **3.2   2 venom** venomous person

SIR ANDREW   Marry, I saw your niece do more favours to the
5   count's servingman than ever she bestowed upon me. I saw't
i'th'orchard.

SIR TOBY   Did she see thee the while, old boy? Tell me that.

SIR ANDREW   As plain as I see you now.

FABIAN   This was a great argument of love in her toward
10   you.

SIR ANDREW   'Slight, will you make an ass o'me?

FABIAN   I will prove it legitimate, sir, upon the oaths of
judgement and reason.

SIR TOBY   And they have been grand-jurymen since before
15   Noah was a sailor.

FABIAN   She did show favour to the youth in your sight only
to exasperate you, to awake your dormouse valour, to put
fire in your heart and brimstone in your liver. You should
then have accosted her, and with some excellent jests, fire-
20   new from the mint, you should have banged the youth into
dumbness. This was looked for at your hand, and this was
balked. The double gilt of this opportunity you let time wash
off, and you are now sailed into the north of my lady's
opinion, where you will hang like an icicle on a Dutchman's
25   beard, unless you do redeem it by some laudable attempt
either of valour or policy.

SIR ANDREW   An't be any way, it must be with valour, for policy I
hate: I had as lief be a Brownist as a politician.

SIR TOBY   Why, then, build me thy fortunes upon the basis of
30   valour. Challenge me the count's youth to fight with him.
Hurt him in eleven places: my niece shall take note of it. And
assure thyself, there is no love-broker in the world can more
prevail in man's commendation with woman than report of
valour.

---

6 i'th'orchard in the garden   **7 the while** at the time   **9 argument** proof   **12 it** my case
oaths sworn testament   **15 Noah** biblical character who survived a mighty flood sent by God
17 dormouse sleepy   **19 fire-new . . . mint** i.e. like a freshly minted coin   **20 banged** struck
22 balked avoided/neglected   **double gilt** i.e. golden (**opportunity**)   **23 north** cold region
26 policy strategy   **28 lief** willingly   **Brownist** follower of Robert Browne, founder of an
extreme puritan sect   **politician** schemer   **29 build me** build   **30 Challenge me** challenge
32 love-broker go-between

35   FABIAN   There is no way but this, Sir Andrew.

       SIR ANDREW   Will either of you bear me a challenge to him?

       SIR TOBY   Go, write it in a martial hand. Be curst and brief: it is
                     no matter how witty, so it be eloquent and full of invention.
                     Taunt him with the licence of ink. If thou thou'st him some
40   thrice, it shall not be amiss. And as many lies as will lie in thy
                     sheet of paper, although the sheet were big enough for the
                     bed of Ware in England, set 'em down. Go, about it. Let there
                     be gall enough in thy ink, though thou write with a goose-
                     pen, no matter. About it.

45   SIR ANDREW   Where shall I find you?

       SIR TOBY   We'll call thee at the *cubiculo*. Go.

                                                              Exit Sir Andrew

       FABIAN   This is a dear manikin to you, Sir Toby.

       SIR TOBY   I have been dear to him, lad, some two thousand
                     strong, or so.

50   FABIAN   We shall have a rare letter from him; but you'll not
                     deliver't?

       SIR TOBY   Never trust me, then. And by all means stir on the
                     youth to an answer. I think oxen and wainropes cannot hale
                     them together. For Andrew, if he were opened and you find
55   so much blood in his liver as will clog the foot of a flea, I'll eat
                     the rest of th'anatomy.

       FABIAN   And his opposite, the youth, bears in his visage no
                     great presage of cruelty.

       Enter Maria

       SIR TOBY   Look where the youngest wren of mine comes.

---

37 martial hand military style/handwriting   **curst** quarrelsome   **38 so** provided that
invention innovation   **39 licence of ink** freedom encouraged by writing rather than speaking
thou'st call him "thou," an insult to a stranger ("you" is the polite form)   **40 lies** accusations
of lying   **42 bed of Ware** famous bed, able to hold twelve people   **43 gall** bile, anger/an
ingredient in ink (oak-gall)   **goose-pen** quill-pen made from a goose's feather (may play on
sense of **goose** as "fool")   **46 *cubiculo*** "bedroom" (Latin)   **47 manikin** little man, puppet
48 dear costly   **two thousand** probably ducats (gold coins)   **50 rare** marvelous, i.e.
entertaining   **53 wainropes** wagon ropes, pulled by **oxen**   **hale** haul, drag   **56 th'anatomy**
i.e. his skeleton/body   **57 opposite** adversary   **visage** appearance/face   **58 presage**
indication   **59 youngest wren** the wren is a small bird (a play on Maria's size); some editors
emend "mine" to "nine"

60	MARIA	If you desire the spleen, and will laugh yourselves into stitches, follow me. Yond gull Malvolio is turned heathen, a very renegado; for there is no Christian that means to be saved by believing rightly can ever believe such impossible passages of grossness. He's in yellow stockings.
65	SIR TOBY	And cross-gartered?
	MARIA	Most villainously: like a pedant that keeps a school i'th'church. I have dogged him like his murderer. He does obey every point of the letter that I dropped to betray him: he does smile his face into more lines than is in the new map with the augmentation of the Indies. You have not seen such a thing as 'tis. I can hardly forbear hurling things at him. I know my lady will strike him. If she do, he'll smile and take't for a great favour.
70		
	SIR TOBY	Come, bring us, bring us where he is. *Exeunt*

Act 3 Scene 3   *running scene 12*

Enter Sebastian and Antonio

SEBASTIAN   I would not by my will have troubled you,
But since you make your pleasure of your pains,
I will no further chide you.

ANTONIO   I could not stay behind you: my desire,
5   More sharp than filèd steel, did spur me forth,
And not all love to see you, though so much
As might have drawn one to a longer voyage,
But jealousy what might befall your travel,
Being skill-less in these parts, which to a stranger,
10   Unguided and unfriended, often prove

---

60 **spleen** fit of laughter (the **spleen** was thought to be the seat of laughter)   61 **gull** fool, dupe
62 **renegado** deserter of his religion   64 **passages of grossness** i.e. the ludicrous statements
in Maria's letter   66 **villainously** offensively, horribly   **pedant** schoolmaster   67 **dogged**
followed closely   69 **new . . . Indies** probably refers to a map published in 1599 that showed
the East Indies in much greater detail than previously   71 **forbear** desist from   3.3   3 **chide**
scold   5 **filèd** sharpened   6 **all** only (out of)   **so much** enough (love)   8 **jealousy** concern,
apprehension (about)   9 **skill-less in** unacquainted with   **stranger** foreigner

Rough and unhospitable. My willing love,
The rather by these arguments of fear,
Set forth in your pursuit.

SEBASTIAN   My kind Antonio,
15   I can no other answer make but thanks,
And thanks, and ever oft good turns
Are shuffled off with such uncurrent pay.
But were my worth, as is my conscience, firm,
You should find better dealing. What's to do?
20   Shall we go see the relics of this town?

ANTONIO   Tomorrow, sir. Best first go see your lodging.

SEBASTIAN   I am not weary, and 'tis long to night.
I pray you let us satisfy our eyes
With the memorials and the things of fame
25   That do renown this city.

ANTONIO   Would you'd pardon me.
I do not without danger walk these streets.
Once in a sea-fight gainst the count his galleys
I did some service, of such note indeed,
30   That were I ta'en here it would scarce be answered.

SEBASTIAN   Belike you slew great number of his people.

ANTONIO   Th'offence is not of such a bloody nature,
Albeit the quality of the time and quarrel
Might well have given us bloody argument.
35   It might have since been answered in repaying
What we took from them, which for traffic's sake,
Most of our city did. Only myself stood out,
For which, if I be lapsèd in this place,
I shall pay dear.

---

12 rather more readily   **16 ever oft** very often   **17 shuffled off** shrugged aside   **uncurrent**
worthless   **18 worth** financial means   **conscience** feeling of obligation   **firm** substantial/
reliable   **19 dealing** treatment/reward   **20 relics** antiquities, old sights   **25 renown** make
famous   **28 count his** count's, i.e. duke's   **galleys** ships usually propelled by oars as well as
sails   **30 it . . . answered** it would be virtually impossible to account for it/make reparation
(i.e. Antonio's life would be in danger)   **31 Belike** presumably   **33 Albeit** even though
34 bloody argument cause for shedding blood   **35 answered** requited   **36 traffic's** trade's
38 lapsèd apprehended/caught out

40	SEBASTIAN	Do not then walk too open.	
	ANTONIO	It doth not fit me. Hold, sir, here's my	*Gives his purse*

purse.

In the south suburbs, at the Elephant,

Is best to lodge. I will bespeak our diet,

Whiles you beguile the time and feed your knowledge

45 With viewing of the town. There shall you have me.

SEBASTIAN Why I your purse?

ANTONIO Haply your eye shall light upon some toy

You have desire to purchase, and your store,

I think, is not for idle markets, sir.

50 SEBASTIAN I'll be your purse-bearer and leave you

For an hour.

ANTONIO To th'Elephant.

SEBASTIAN I do remember. *Exeunt*

Act 3 Scene 4 *running scene 13*

Enter Olivia and Maria

OLIVIA I have sent after him: he says he'll come. *Aside*

How shall I feast him? What bestow of him?

For youth is bought more oft than begged or borrowed.

I speak too loud.—

5 Where's Malvolio? He is sad and civil,

And suits well for a servant with my fortunes.

Where is Malvolio?

MARIA He's coming, madam, but in very strange manner.

He is sure possessed, madam.

10 OLIVIA Why, what's the matter? Does he rave?

MARIA No, madam, he does nothing but smile: your
ladyship were best to have some guard about you, if he
come, for sure the man is tainted in's wits.

---

40 **open** publicly   41 **doth not fit** does not suit/is not appropriate for   42 **Elephant** name of
an inn   43 **bespeak our diet** order our food   44 **beguile** while away   45 **have** meet
47 **Haply** perhaps   **toy** trifle   48 **store** available money   49 **idle markets** trivial purchases
3.4   1 him i.e. Cesario   **2 of** on   **5 sad** serious   **civil** decorous   **9 possessed** by evil spirits,
i.e. mad

OLIVIA   Go call him hither.— I am as mad as he, *Maria goes to*
15   If sad and merry madness equal be.   *call Malvolio*

Enter Malvolio [cross-gartered and in yellow stockings]

How now, Malvolio?

MALVOLIO   Sweet lady, ho, ho.

OLIVIA   Smilest thou? I sent for thee upon a sad occasion.

MALVOLIO   Sad, lady? I could be sad: this does make some
20   obstruction in the blood, this cross-gartering, but what of
that? If it please the eye of one, it is with me as the very true
sonnet is, 'Please one, and please all'.

OLIVIA   Why, how dost thou, man? What is the matter with
thee?

25   MALVOLIO   Not black in my mind, though yellow in my legs. It
did come to his hands, and commands shall be executed. I
think we do know the sweet Roman hand.

OLIVIA   Wilt thou go to bed, Malvolio?

MALVOLIO   To bed? Ay, sweetheart, and I'll come to thee.

30   OLIVIA   God comfort thee! Why dost thou smile so and kiss
thy hand so oft?

MARIA   How do you, Malvolio?

MALVOLIO   At your request! Yes, nightingales answer daws.

MARIA   Why appear you with this ridiculous boldness
35   before my lady?

MALVOLIO   'Be not afraid of greatness.' 'Twas well writ.

OLIVIA   What meanest thou by that, Malvolio?

MALVOLIO   'Some are born great'—

OLIVIA   Ha?

40   MALVOLIO   'Some achieve greatness'—

OLIVIA   What say'st thou?

MALVOLIO   'And some have greatness thrust upon them.'

OLIVIA   Heaven restore thee!

---

19 sad serious/melancholy   **22 sonnet** song/poem   **'Please . . . all'** a ballad about women
having their own way sexually   **25 black** melancholic (from an excess of black bile)   **It** i.e.
the letter   **26 his** i.e. Malvolio's   **27 Roman hand** fashionable Italian style of handwriting
28 go to bed i.e. to rest (but Malvolio takes this as sexually suggestive)   **30 kiss thy hand** a
fashionable greeting among courtiers   **33 daws** jackdaws, birds of the crow family/fools

	MALVOLIO	'Remember who commended thy yellow stockings'—
45	OLIVIA	Thy yellow stockings?
	MALVOLIO	'And wished to see thee cross-gartered.'
	OLIVIA	Cross-gartered?
	MALVOLIO	'Go to, thou art made, if thou desirest to be so'—
	OLIVIA	Am I made?
50	MALVOLIO	'If not, let me see thee a servant still.'
	OLIVIA	Why, this is very midsummer madness.

Enter Servant

SERVANT   Madam, the young gentleman of the count Orsino's is returned. I could hardly entreat him back. He attends your ladyship's pleasure.

55 OLIVIA   I'll come to him.   [*Exit Servant*]
Good Maria, let this fellow be looked to. Where's my cousin Toby? Let some of my people have a special care of him. I would not have him miscarry for the half of my dowry.

Exeunt [Olivia and Maria]

MALVOLIO   O, ho! Do you come near me now? No worse man
60   than Sir Toby to look to me! This concurs directly with the letter: she sends him on purpose that I may appear stubborn to him, for she incites me to that in the letter. 'Cast thy humble slough,' says she, 'be opposite with a kinsman, surly with servants, let thy tongue tang with arguments of state,
65   put thyself into the trick of singularity.' And consequently sets down the manner how: as, a sad face, a reverend carriage, a slow tongue, in the habit of some sir of note, and so forth. I have limed her, but it is Jove's doing, and Jove make me thankful. And when she went away now, 'Let this fellow
70   be looked to.' Fellow? Not Malvolio, nor after my degree, but fellow. Why, everything adheres together, that no dram of a

---

51 **midsummer** proverbially the season for **madness**   53 **hardly** with difficulty   **attends** awaits   58 **miscarry** come to harm   59 **come near** begin to understand/appreciate   65 **consequently** subsequently   66 **reverend carriage** dignified bearing   67 **habit** manner/ clothing   **sir of note** distinguished man   68 **limed** caught; birdlime was a sticky substance smeared on branches to trap birds   70 **Fellow** equal   **after my degree** according to my position   71 **dram** tiny amount

scruple, no scruple of a scruple, no obstacle, no incredulous
or unsafe circumstance — What can be said? Nothing that
can be can come between me and the full prospect of my
75 hopes. Well, Jove, not I, is the doer of this, and he is to be
thanked.

Enter Toby, Fabian and Maria

SIR TOBY   Which way is he, in the name of sanctity? If all the
devils of hell be drawn in little, and Legion himself possessed
him, yet I'll speak to him.

80 FABIAN   Here he is, here he is. How is't with you, sir? How
is't with you, man?

MALVOLIO   Go off. I discard you. Let me enjoy my private. Go off.

MARIA   Lo, how hollow the fiend speaks within him! Did not
I tell you? Sir Toby, my lady prays you to have a care of him.

85 MALVOLIO   Ah, ha, does she so?

SIR TOBY   Go to, go to. Peace, peace. We must deal gently with
him. Let me alone.— How do you, Malvolio? How is't with
you? What, man, defy the devil! Consider, he's an enemy to
mankind.

90 MALVOLIO   Do you know what you say?

MARIA   La you, an you speak ill of the devil, how he takes it
at heart! Pray God, he be not bewitched!

FABIAN   Carry his water to th'wise woman.

MARIA   Marry, and it shall be done tomorrow morning, if I
95 live. My lady would not lose him for more than I'll say.

MALVOLIO   How now, mistress?

MARIA   O Lord!

SIR TOBY   Prithee hold thy peace, this is not the way. Do you
not see you move him? Let me alone with him.

---

72 **scruple** small quantity/doubt   **incredulous** incredible   73 **unsafe** unreliable   78 **drawn
in little** gathered in a small space/painted in miniature   **Legion** biblical reference to a
multitude of devils; Sir Toby may mistakenly think it is the name of a specific devil   82 **private**
privacy, with possible play on "private parts"   83 **Lo** look   **hollow** echoingly   84 **have a
take**   87 **Let me alone** leave him to me   91 **La** look   93 **water** urine, examined for diagnosis
wise woman local healer, thought able to cure those bewitched   99 **move** excite/provoke

100 FABIAN	No way but gentleness, gently, gently. The fiend is rough, and will not be roughly used.
SIR TOBY	Why, how now, my bawcock? How dost thou, chuck?
MALVOLIO	Sir!
105 SIR TOBY	Ay, Biddy, come with me. What, man, 'tis not for gravity to play at cherry-pit with Satan. Hang him, foul collier!
MARIA	Get him to say his prayers, good Sir Toby, get him to pray.
110 MALVOLIO	My prayers, minx?
MARIA	No, I warrant you he will not hear of godliness.
MALVOLIO	Go, hang yourselves all! You are idle shallow things. I am not of your element. You shall know more hereafter.

Exit

SIR TOBY	Is't possible?
115 FABIAN	If this were played upon a stage now, I could condemn it as an improbable fiction.
SIR TOBY	His very genius hath taken the infection of the device, man.
MARIA	Nay, pursue him now, lest the device take air and 120 ·taint.
FABIAN	Why, we shall make him mad indeed.
MARIA	The house will be the quieter.
SIR TOBY	Come, we'll have him in a dark room and bound. My niece is already in the belief that he's mad. We may carry 125 it thus, for our pleasure and his penance, till our very pastime, tired out of breath, prompt us to have mercy on him, at which time we will bring the device to the bar and crown thee for a finder of madmen. But see, but see.

---

102 bawcock good fellow (from the French *beau coq*, i.e. "fine bird")   **103 chuck** chick
105 Biddy hen   **106 gravity** respectability   **cherry-pit** children's game in which cherry-stones are thrown into a hole   **foul collier** dirty coalman, i.e. the devil   **112 idle** worthless/trivial   **113 element** sphere/type   **117 genius** soul/guardian spirit   **119 take . . . taint** be spoiled (by exposure to air)   **123 in . . . bound** conventional treatment for the insane
124 carry manage/maintain   **127 bar** open court, i.e. judgment   **128 finder of madmen** juror who formally declared whether a man was mad

Enter Sir Andrew

FABIAN   More matter for a May morning.

130   SIR ANDREW   Here's the challenge, read it. I warrant   *Shows a paper*
      there's vinegar and pepper in't.

FABIAN   Is't so saucy?

SIR ANDREW   Ay, is't, I warrant him. Do but read.

SIR TOBY   Give me. 'Youth, whatsoever thou art, thou   *Reads*
135   art but a scurvy fellow.'

FABIAN   Good, and valiant.

SIR TOBY   'Wonder not, nor admire not in thy mind,   *Reads*
      why I do call thee so, for I will show thee no reason for't.'

FABIAN   A good note, that keeps you from the blow of the
140   law.

SIR TOBY   'Thou comest to the lady Olivia, and in my   *Reads*
      sight she uses thee kindly. But thou liest in thy throat, that is
      not the matter I challenge thee for.'

FABIAN   Very brief, and to exceeding good sense— less.   *Aside*

145   SIR TOBY   'I will waylay thee going home, where if it   *Reads*
      be thy chance to kill me'—

FABIAN   Good.

SIR TOBY   'Thou killest me like a rogue and a villain.'   *Reads*

FABIAN   Still you keep o'th'windy side of the law. Good.

150   SIR TOBY   'Fare thee well, and God have mercy upon   *Reads*
      one of our souls! He may have mercy upon mine, but my
      hope is better, and so look to thyself. Thy friend, as thou usest
      him, and thy sworn enemy,

                                    Andrew Aguecheek.'

155   If this letter move him not, his legs cannot. I'll give't him.

MARIA   You may have very fit occasion for't: he is now in
      some commerce with my lady, and will by and by depart.

SIR TOBY   Go, Sir Andrew. Scout me for him at the corner of

---

129 matter substance/sport   May morning i.e. festive time   130 warrant assure you/confirm
132 saucy spicy/insolent   133 warrant assure   135 scurvy worthless/contemptible
137 admire marvel   139 note remark   keeps protects   blow . . . law legal punishment
(for breaching the peace)   142 liest . . . throat lie outrageously   149 o'th'windy on the
windward, i.e. safe   152 hope i.e. of success   as . . . him insofar as you treat him as such
155 move provoke/set in motion   157 commerce transaction/conversational exchange
158 Scout me keep watch (for me)

the orchard like a bumbaily: so soon as ever thou see'st him,
160 draw, and as thou draw'st swear horrible, for it comes to pass
oft that a terrible oath, with a swaggering accent sharply
twanged off, gives manhood more approbation than ever
proof itself would have earned him. Away!

SIR ANDREW   Nay, let me alone for swearing.   *Exit*

165 SIR TOBY   Now will not I deliver his letter, for the behaviour of
the young gentleman gives him out to be of good capacity
and breeding. His employment between his lord and my
niece confirms no less: therefore this letter, being so
excellently ignorant, will breed no terror in the youth. He
170 will find it comes from a clodpole. But, sir, I will deliver his
challenge by word of mouth; set upon Aguecheek a notable
report of valour, and drive the gentleman, as I know his
youth will aptly receive it, into a most hideous opinion of his
rage, skill, fury and impetuosity. This will so fright them both
175 that they will kill one another by the look, like cockatrices.

Enter Olivia and Viola

FABIAN   Here he comes with your niece. Give them way till
he take leave, and presently after him.

SIR TOBY   I will meditate the while upon some horrid message
for a challenge.

[*Exeunt Sir Toby, Fabian and Maria*]

180 OLIVIA   I have said too much unto a heart of stone
And laid mine honour too unchary on't.
There's something in me that reproves my fault,
But such a headstrong potent fault it is,
That it but mocks reproof.

185 VIOLA   With the same 'haviour that your passion bears
Goes on my master's griefs.

---

159 bumbaily bailiff who crept up on the debtor from behind   **160 horrible** terribly/
exceedingly   **162 twanged off** uttered ringingly/said with a snide nasal intonation
approbation credit   **163 proof** testing out   **164 let me alone** i.e. you can rely on me
166 capacity intelligence   **170 clodpole** idiot   **173 youth** inexperience   **aptly receive**
readily believe   **hideous** terrifying   **175 cockatrices** basilisks, mythical reptiles whose gaze
had the power to kill   **176 Give them way** keep out of their way   **177 presently** immediately
178 horrid terrifying   **181 laid** laid down/exposed   **unchary** carelessly   **185 'haviour . . .
bears** behavior that characterizes your passion

OLIVIA   Here, wear this jewel for me, 'tis my picture.
Refuse it not. It hath no tongue to vex you.
And I beseech you come again tomorrow.
190   What shall you ask of me that I'll deny,
That honour saved may upon asking give?

VIOLA   Nothing but this: your true love for my master.

OLIVIA   How with mine honour may I give him that
Which I have given to you?

195   VIOLA   I will acquit you.

OLIVIA   Well, come again tomorrow. Fare thee well.
A fiend like thee might bear my soul to hell.   [*Exit*]

Enter Toby and Fabian

SIR TOBY   Gentleman, God save thee.

VIOLA   And you, sir.

200   SIR TOBY   That defence thou hast, betake thee to't. Of what
nature the wrongs are thou hast done him, I know not, but
thy intercepter, full of despite, bloody as the hunter, attends
thee at the orchard-end. Dismount thy tuck, be yare in thy
preparation, for thy assailant is quick, skilful and deadly.

205   VIOLA   You mistake, sir, I am sure. No man hath any
quarrel to me: my remembrance is very free and clear from
any image of offence done to any man.

SIR TOBY   You'll find it otherwise, I assure you: therefore, if
you hold your life at any price, betake you to your guard, for
210   your opposite hath in him what youth, strength, skill and
wrath can furnish man withal.

VIOLA   I pray you, sir, what is he?

SIR TOBY   He is knight, dubbed with unhatched rapier and on
carpet consideration, but he is a devil in private brawl. Souls
215   and bodies hath he divorced three, and his incensement at

---

187 **jewel** piece of jewelry, here a miniature portrait of Olivia   191 **honour saved** i.e. apart
from my virginity   195 **acquit** excuse, release (from obligation to love)   200 **That** whatever
betake resort   202 **intercepter** one lying in wait   **despite** contempt   **bloody** bloodthirsty
203 **Dismount** draw   **tuck** sword   **yare** quick   206 **to** with   **remembrance** memory
209 **price** value   210 **opposite** opponent   211 **withal** with   213 **dubbed** invested with
knightly status   **unhatched** unhacked, unmarked (in battle)   **on carpet consideration** for
courtly, rather than military, reasons   215 **incensement** fury

this moment is so implacable that satisfaction can be none but by pangs of death and sepulchre. Hob, nob, is his word: give't or take't.

VIOLA   I will return again into the house and desire some
220   conduct of the lady. I am no fighter. I have heard of some kind of men that put quarrels purposely on others, to taste their valour. Belike this is a man of that quirk.

SIR TOBY   Sir, no. His indignation derives itself out of a very competent injury: therefore, get you on and give him his
225   desire. Back you shall not to the house, unless you undertake that with me which with as much safety you might answer him: therefore, on, or strip your sword stark naked, for meddle you must, that's certain, or forswear to wear iron about you.

230   VIOLA   This is as uncivil as strange. I beseech you do me this courteous office, as to know of the knight what my offence to him is. It is something of my negligence, nothing of my purpose.

SIR TOBY   I will do so. Signior Fabian, stay you by this
235   gentleman till my return.   *Exit Toby*

VIOLA   Pray you, sir, do you know of this matter?

FABIAN   I know the knight is incensed against you, even to a mortal arbitrement, but nothing of the circumstance more.

VIOLA   I beseech you what manner of man is he?

240   FABIAN   Nothing of that wonderful promise, to read him by his form, as you are like to find him in the proof of his valour. He is, indeed, sir, the most skilful, bloody and fatal opposite that you could possibly have found in any part of Illyria. Will you walk towards him? I will make your peace with him if I
245   can.

---

216 **satisfaction** recompense for offense to one's honor   217 **sepulchre** tomb   **Hob, nob** have or have not, i.e. come what may   **word** motto   220 **conduct** protection   221 **taste** test   222 **quirk** peculiarity   224 **competent** sufficient   226 **that** i.e. the duel   228 **meddle** get involved   **forswear . . . you** cease to wear a sword   231 **office** task   **know of** inquire from   238 **mortal arbitrement** fight to the death   240 **Nothing . . . promise** not at all as extraordinary   **read** judge   241 **form** appearance   **like** likely

VIOLA   I shall be much bound to you for't: I am one that
had rather go with sir priest than sir knight. I care not who
knows so much of my mettle.   *Exeunt*

Enter Toby and Andrew

SIR TOBY   Why, man, he's a very devil. I have not seen such a
250   firago. I had a pass with him, rapier, scabbard and all, and he
gives me the stuck in with such a mortal motion that it is
inevitable. And on the answer, he pays you as surely as your
feet hits the ground they step on. They say he has been
fencer to the Sophy.

255   SIR ANDREW   Pox on't, I'll not meddle with him.

SIR TOBY   Ay, but he will not now be pacified. Fabian can
scarce hold him yonder.

SIR ANDREW   Plague on't, an I thought he had been valiant and
so cunning in fence, I'd have seen him damned ere I'd have
260   challenged him. Let him let the matter slip, and I'll give him
my horse, grey Capilet.

SIR TOBY   I'll make the motion. Stand here, make a good show
on't.— This shall end without the perdition of souls.   *Aside*
Marry, I'll ride your horse as well as I ride you.

Enter Fabian and Viola

265   I have his horse to take up the quarrel. I have   *Aside to Fabian*
persuaded him the youth's a devil.

FABIAN   He is as horribly conceited of him, and pants and
looks pale, as if a bear were at his heels.

SIR TOBY   There's no remedy, sir, he will fight with   *To Viola*
270   you for's oath sake. Marry, he hath better bethought him of
his quarrel, and he finds that now scarce to be worth talking
of: therefore draw for the supportance of his vow. He protests
he will not hurt you.

---

248 **mettle** spirit/courage   250 **firago** virago, female fighter   **pass** bout (of fencing)
251 **stuck in** fencing thrust   **mortal** fatal   **motion** fencing maneuver   252 **inevitable**
unavoidable   **answer** return hit   **pays you** strikes you in return   254 **to** in the service of
Sophy Shah of Persia   255 **Pox** plague   257 **hold** restrain   259 **cunning** skillful   **fence**
fencing   **ere** before   262 **motion** offer   263 **perdition of souls** i.e. loss of life   **perdition**
destruction, damnation   264 **ride** i.e. make a fool of   265 **take up** settle   267 **horribly**
conceited has just as terrifying an idea   270 **for's oath** for his oath's   271 **quarrel** cause of
complaint   272 **supportance** upholding   **protests** declares/vows

VIOLA	Pray God defend me! A little thing would	*Aside*

275 make me tell them how much I lack of a man.

FABIAN   Give ground if you see him furious.   *To Viola*

SIR TOBY   Come, Sir Andrew, there's no remedy. The gentleman
will, for his honour's sake, have one bout with you. He cannot
by the duello avoid it. But he has promised me, as he is a
280 gentleman and a soldier, he will not hurt you. Come on, to't.

SIR ANDREW   Pray God he keep his oath!

Enter Antonio

VIOLA   I do assure you, 'tis against my will.   *To Fabian/They draw*

ANTONIO   Put up your sword. If this young   *their swords*
gentleman

Have done offence, I take the fault on me.

285 If you offend him, I for him defy you.

SIR TOBY   You, sir? Why, what are you?

ANTONIO   One, sir, that for his love dares yet do more
Than you have heard him brag to you he will.

SIR TOBY   Nay, if you be an undertaker, I am for you.   *They draw*

Enter Officers

290 FABIAN   O, good Sir Toby, hold! Here come the officers.

SIR TOBY   I'll be with you anon.   *To Antonio*

VIOLA   Pray, sir, put your sword up, if you please.   *To Sir Andrew*

SIR ANDREW   Marry, will I, sir. And for that I promised you, I'll be
as good as my word. He will bear you easily and reins well.

295 FIRST OFFICER   This is the man; do thy office.   *Indicates Antonio*

SECOND OFFICER   Antonio, I arrest thee at the suit of Count
Orsino.

ANTONIO   You do mistake me, sir.

FIRST OFFICER   No, sir, no jot. I know your favour well,
300 Though now you have no sea-cap on your head.
Take him away: he knows I know him well.

---

274 A . . . would it wouldn't take much to (**thing** plays on the sense of "penis")   **279 duello**
established dueling code   **283 up** away   **289 undertaker** one who takes on a task/challenger
for ready for   **291 anon** shortly   **293 for that** as for what   **294 He** i.e. Capilet, the horse
reins is obedient, responds to the reins   **296 suit** order/request   **299 favour** face

ANTONIO   I must obey.— This comes with seeking you.   *To Viola*
But there's no remedy, I shall answer it.
What will you do, now my necessity
305   Makes me to ask you for my purse? It grieves me
Much more for what I cannot do for you
Than what befalls myself. You stand amazed;
But be of comfort.

SECOND OFFICER   Come, sir, away.

310   ANTONIO   I must entreat of you some of that money.   *To Viola*

VIOLA   What money, sir?
For the fair kindness you have showed me here,
And part being prompted by your present trouble,
Out of my lean and low ability
315   I'll lend you something. My having is not much.
I'll make division of my present with you.
Hold, there's half my coffer.   *Offers money*

ANTONIO   Will you deny me now?
Is't possible that my deserts to you
320   Can lack persuasion? Do not tempt my misery,
Lest that it make me so unsound a man
As to upbraid you with those kindnesses
That I have done for you.

VIOLA   I know of none,
325   Nor know I you by voice or any feature.
I hate ingratitude more in a man
Than lying, vainness, babbling, drunkenness,
Or any taint of vice whose strong corruption
Inhabits our frail blood.

330   ANTONIO   O heavens themselves!

SECOND OFFICER   Come, sir, I pray you go.

ANTONIO   Let me speak a little. This youth that you see here
I snatched one half out of the jaws of death,

---

303 **answer** be accountable for   307 **amazed** shocked/bewildered   313 **part** in part
315 **having** fortune   316 **present** available resources   317 **coffer** money   318 **deny**
reject/disown   319 **deserts** worthy deeds   320 **lack persuasion** fail to persuade you to help
me   **tempt** try   321 **unsound** morally weak/inadequate   327 **vainness** ostentation

Relieved him with such sanctity of love,
335 And to his image, which methought did promise
Most venerable worth, did I devotion.

FIRST OFFICER   What's that to us? The time goes by. Away!

ANTONIO   But O, how vile an idol proves this god.
Thou hast, Sebastian, done good feature shame.
340 In nature there's no blemish but the mind.
None can be called deformed but the unkind.
Virtue is beauty, but the beauteous evil
Are empty trunks o'erflourished by the devil.

FIRST OFFICER   The man grows mad. Away with him! Come,
345 come, sir.

ANTONIO   Lead me on.   *Exit [with Officers]*

VIOLA   Methinks his words do from such passion fly,   *Aside*
That he believes himself, so do not I.
Prove true, imagination, O, prove true,
350 That I, dear brother, be now ta'en for you!

SIR TOBY   Come hither, knight. Come hither, Fabian. We'll
whisper o'er a couplet or two of most sage   *They stand aside*
saws.

VIOLA   He named Sebastian. I my brother know
355 Yet living in my glass, even such and so
In favour was my brother, and he went
Still in this fashion, colour, ornament,
For him I imitate. O, if it prove,
Tempests are kind and salt waves fresh in love.   *[Exit]*

360 SIR TOBY   A very dishonest paltry boy, and more a coward
than a hare. His dishonesty appears in leaving his friend
here in necessity and denying him. And for his cowardship,
ask Fabian.

---

334 **sanctity** holiness   335 **image** appearance (plays on the sense of "religious icon")
336 **venerable worth** worthy to be venerated   339 **feature** physical appearance   341 **unkind**
cruel/unnatural   343 **trunks** chests/bodies   **o'erflourished** richly decorated/made
outwardly beautiful   352 **sage** solemn/dignified   353 **saws** sayings   355 **glass** mirrored
reflection/image   356 **favour** appearance   **went** went about   357 **Still** always   **ornament**
clothing, adornments   358 **prove** i.e. to be true   360 **dishonest** dishonorable   **a coward**
cowardly

FABIAN	A coward, a most devout coward, religious in it.
365 SIR ANDREW	'Slid, I'll after him again and beat him.
SIR TOBY	Do, cuff him soundly, but never draw thy sword.
SIR ANDREW	An I do not—
FABIAN	Come, let's see the event.
SIR TOBY	I dare lay any money 'twill be nothing yet.

Exeunt

Act 4 Scene 1   *running scene 14*

Enter Sebastian and Clown [Feste]

FESTE   Will you make me believe that I am not sent for you?

SEBASTIAN   Go to, go to, thou art a foolish fellow.
Let me be clear of thee.

FESTE   Well held out, i'faith! No, I do not know you, nor I
5   am not sent to you by my lady, to bid you come speak with
her, nor your name is not Master Cesario, nor this is not my
nose neither. Nothing that is so is so.

SEBASTIAN   I prithee vent thy folly somewhere else. Thou
know'st not me.

10   FESTE   Vent my folly! He has heard that word of some great
man and now applies it to a fool. Vent my folly! I am afraid
this great lubber the world will prove a cockney. I prithee
now ungird thy strangeness and tell me what I shall vent to
my lady. Shall I vent to her that thou art coming?

15   SEBASTIAN   I prithee, foolish Greek, depart   *Gives money*
from me. There's money for thee. If you tarry longer, I shall
give worse payment.

FESTE   By my troth, thou hast an open hand. These wise
men that give fools money get themselves a good report —
20   after fourteen years' purchase.

---

364 religious devout   **365 'Slid** by God's eyelid (common oath)   **368 event** outcome
369 yet after all   **4.1**   **4 held out** kept up   **8 vent** utter, let out   **10 of** from   **12 lubber**
clumsy idiot   **cockney** pampered child/affected, effeminate fellow   **13 ungird** take off
strangeness aloofness   **15 Greek** buffoon/speaker of gibberish   **16 tarry** linger   **17 worse**
payment i.e. blows   **18 open** generous (with money or blows)   **19 report** reputation
20 fourteen years' purchase i.e. a large investment of time and money

Enter Andrew, Toby and Fabian

SIR ANDREW   Now, sir, have I met you again?   *Strikes Sebastian*
There's for you.

SEBASTIAN   Why, there's for thee, and there, and   *Beats Sir Andrew*
there. Are all the people mad?

25   SIR TOBY   Hold, sir, or I'll throw your dagger o'er the house.

FESTE   This will I tell my lady straight. I would not be in
some of your coats for twopence.   *[Exit]*

SIR TOBY   Come on, sir, hold.

SIR ANDREW   Nay, let him alone. I'll go another way to work with
30   him. I'll have an action of battery against him, if there be
any law in Illyria. Though I struck him first, yet it's no
matter for that.

SEBASTIAN   Let go thy hand.

SIR TOBY   Come, sir, I will not let you go. Come, my young
35   soldier, put up your iron. You are well fleshed. Come on.

SEBASTIAN   I will be free from thee. What wouldst thou now? If
thou darest tempt me further, draw thy sword.

SIR TOBY   What, what? Nay, then I must have an ounce or two
of this malapert blood from you.

Enter Olivia

40   OLIVIA   Hold, Toby. On thy life I charge thee, hold!

SIR TOBY   Madam!

OLIVIA   Will it be ever thus? Ungracious wretch,
Fit for the mountains and the barbarous caves,
Where manners ne'er were preached! Out of my sight!—
45   Be not offended, dear Cesario.—
Rudesby, be gone!

[Exeunt Sir Toby, Sir Andrew and Fabian]
I prithee, gentle friend,
Let thy fair wisdom, not thy passion, sway
In this uncivil and unjust extent
Against thy peace. Go with me to my house,

---

26 **straight** at once   26 **in . . . coats** in your position   28 **hold** restrain yourself
30 **action of battery** lawsuit for assault   35 **iron** dagger/sword   **fleshed** initiated into
fighting   39 **malapert** impudent   46 **Rudesby** ruffian   **friend** friend/lover   48 **uncivil**
barbarous   **extent** assault

50   And hear thou there how many fruitless pranks
        This ruffian hath botched up, that thou thereby
        Mayst smile at this. Thou shalt not choose but go.
        Do not deny. Beshrew his soul for me,
        He started one poor heart of mine in thee.

55 SEBASTIAN   What relish is in this? How runs the stream?   *Aside*
        Or I am mad, or else this is a dream.
        Let fancy still my sense in Lethe steep.
        If it be thus to dream, still let me sleep!

    OLIVIA   Nay, come, I prithee. Would thou'dst be ruled by me!
60 SEBASTIAN   Madam, I will.

    OLIVIA   O, say so, and so be!   *Exeunt*

Act 4 Scene 2   *running scene 15*

Enter Maria and Clown [Feste]

    MARIA   Nay, I prithee put on this gown and this   *Hands him a*
        beard. Make him believe thou art Sir Topas   *gown and beard*
        the curate. Do it quickly. I'll call Sir Toby the whilst.   *[Exit]*

    FESTE   Well, I'll put it on, and I will dissemble myself in't,
5   and I would I were the first that ever dissembled in such a
        gown. I am not tall enough to become the   *Puts on gown*
        function well, nor lean enough to be thought a   *and beard*
        good student. But to be said an honest man and a good
        housekeeper goes as fairly as to say a careful man and a great
10   scholar. The competitors enter.

Enter Toby [and Maria]

    SIR TOBY   Jove bless thee, Master Parson.

---

51 **botched up** patched together   53 **Beshrew** curse   54 **started** startled/drove from cover
heart puns on "hart"   55 **relish** meaning (literally, "taste")   56 **Or** either   57 **fancy**
imagination   **Lethe** river of forgetfulness in the classical underworld   58 **still** always
59 **Would thou'dst** if only you would   **4.2**   2 **Sir** respectful title for priest   **Topas** topaz, a
precious stone, was supposed to cure madness; also proverbial for a puritan priest   3 **curate**
parish priest   **the whilst** in the meantime   4 **dissemble** disguise   5 **dissembled** feigned,
deceived   6 **become** suit   7 **function** task/role (of priest)   8 **said** reputed   9 **housekeeper**
host   **goes as fairly** sounds as good   **careful** painstaking/conscientious   10 **competitors**
conspirators, partners in crime

FESTE   *Bonos dies*, Sir Toby. For, as the old hermit of Prague that never saw pen and ink very wittily said to a niece of King Gorboduc, 'That that is, is.' So I, being Master Parson, am Master Parson; for what is 'that' but 'that', and 'is' but 'is'?

SIR TOBY   To him, Sir Topas.

FESTE   What, ho, I say? Peace in this prison.

SIR TOBY   The knave counterfeits well, a good knave.

MALVOLIO   Who calls there?   *Within*

FESTE   Sir Topas the curate, who comes to visit Malvolio the lunatic.

MALVOLIO   Sir Topas, Sir Topas, good Sir Topas, go to my lady.

FESTE   Out, hyperbolical fiend! How vexest thou this man! Talkest thou nothing but of ladies?

SIR TOBY   Well said, Master Parson.

MALVOLIO   Sir Topas, never was man thus wronged. Good Sir Topas, do not think I am mad. They have laid me here in hideous darkness.

FESTE   Fie, thou dishonest Satan! I call thee by the most modest terms, for I am one of those gentle ones that will use the devil himself with courtesy. Sayest thou that house is dark?

MALVOLIO   As hell, Sir Topas.

FESTE   Why it hath bay windows transparent as barricadoes, and the clerestories toward the south north are as lustrous as ebony, and yet complainest thou of obstruction?

MALVOLIO   I am not mad, Sir Topas. I say to you, this house is dark.

FESTE   Madman, thou errest. I say there is no darkness but ignorance, in which thou art more puzzled than the Egyptians in their fog.

---

12 *Bonos dies* "good day" (mock Latin/Spanish)   **old . . . Prague** an invented authority
13 never . . . ink was illiterate   **King Gorboduc** legendary British king   **23 hyperbolical** immoderate/vehement/raging   **fiend** evil spirit (supposedly possessing Malvolio)   **vexest** torment   **30 modest terms** mild expressions   **31 house** i.e. room   **35 barricadoes** barricades   **clerestories** upper windows   **41 puzzled** bewildered   **42 Egyptians . . . fog** in the Bible, God punished the Egyptians with three days of darkness

MALVOLIO   I say, this house is as dark as ignorance, though ignorance were as dark as hell; and I say there was never man thus abused. I am no more mad than you are. Make the trial of it in any constant question.

FESTE   What is the opinion of Pythagoras concerning wild fowl?

MALVOLIO   That the soul of our grandam might happily inhabit a bird.

FESTE   What think'st thou of his opinion?

MALVOLIO   I think nobly of the soul, and no way approve his opinion.

FESTE   Fare thee well. Remain thou still in darkness. Thou shalt hold th'opinion of Pythagoras ere I will allow of thy wits, and fear to kill a woodcock, lest thou dispossess the soul of thy grandam. Fare thee well.

MALVOLIO   Sir Topas, Sir Topas!

SIR TOBY   My most exquisite Sir Topas!

FESTE   Nay, I am for all waters.

MARIA   Thou mightst have done this without thy beard and gown. He sees thee not.

SIR TOBY   To him in thine own voice, and bring me word how thou findest him. I would we were well rid of this knavery. If he may be conveniently delivered, I would he were, for I am now so far in offence with my niece that I cannot pursue with any safety this sport to the upshot. Come by and by to my chamber.

Exeunt [Sir Toby and Maria]

FESTE   'Hey, Robin, jolly Robin,   *Sings*
Tell me how thy lady does.'

MALVOLIO   Fool!

---

45 abused wronged/maltreated   **46 constant** decided/consistent/logical   **question** discussion, debate   **47 Pythagoras** ancient Greek philosopher who believed in the transmigration of souls from humans to animals   **49 grandam** grandmother   **happily** perhaps (though may play on adverbial sense)   **55 allow . . . wits** acknowledge you are sane   **56 woodcock** proverbially stupid and easily caught bird   **59 exquisite** ingenious/exact (in imitation)   **60 am . . . waters** can turn my hand to anything   **63 To** go to   **65 delivered** liberated   **67 upshot** final stroke, conclusion   **by and by** straight away

	FESTE	'My lady is unkind, perdy.'	*Sings*
	MALVOLIO	Fool!	
	FESTE	'Alas, why is she so?'	*Sings*
75	MALVOLIO	Fool, I say!	
	FESTE	'She loves another'— Who calls, ha?	*Sings*

MALVOLIO Good fool, as ever thou wilt deserve well at my hand, help me to a candle, and pen, ink and paper. As I am a gentleman, I will live to be thankful to thee for't.

80 FESTE Master Malvolio?

MALVOLIO Ay, good fool.

FESTE Alas, sir, how fell you besides your five wits?

MALVOLIO Fool, there was never man so notoriously abused. I am as well in my wits, fool, as thou art.

85 FESTE But as well? Then you are mad indeed, if you be no better in your wits than a fool.

MALVOLIO They have here propertied me, keep me in darkness, send ministers to me, asses, and do all they can to face me out of my wits.

90 FESTE Advise you what you say. The minister is here.— Malvolio, Malvolio, thy wits the heavens restore!   *As Sir Topas* Endeavour thyself to sleep, and leave thy vain bibble babble.

MALVOLIO Sir Topas!

FESTE Maintain no words with him, good   *As Sir Topas*
95 fellow.— Who, I, sir? Not I, sir. God buy you, good   *As himself*
Sir Topas.—
Marry, amen.—   *As Sir Topas*
I will, sir, I will.   *As himself*

MALVOLIO Fool, fool, fool, I say!

100 FESTE Alas, sir, be patient. What say you, sir? I am shent for speaking to you.

---

72 perdy by God (from French *par dieu*)   **82 besides** out of   **five wits** mental faculties: common sense, fantasy, judgment, memory, and imagination   **83 notoriously** evidently/ outrageously   **85 But** only   **87 propertied** packed away like a piece of furniture/a stage prop   **88 face** bully   **90 Advise you** be careful/consider   **92 bibble babble** idle chatter   **95 God buy you** goodbye, literally "God be with you"   **100 shent** rebuked

MALVOLIO   Good fool, help me to some light and some paper. I
tell thee I am as well in my wits as any man in Illyria.

FESTE   Well-a-day that you were, sir.

105 MALVOLIO   By this hand, I am. Good fool, some ink, paper and
light, and convey what I will set down to my lady. It shall
advantage thee more than ever the bearing of letter did.

FESTE   I will help you to't. But tell me true, are you not mad
indeed? Or do you but counterfeit?

110 MALVOLIO   Believe me, I am not. I tell thee true.

FESTE   Nay, I'll ne'er believe a madman till I see his brains.
I will fetch you light and paper and ink.

MALVOLIO   Fool, I'll requite it in the highest degree. I prithee be
gone.

115 FESTE   I am gone, sir,
And anon, sir,   *Sings*
I'll be with you again,
In a trice,
Like to the old Vice,
120 Your need to sustain,
Who, with dagger of lath,
In his rage and his wrath,
Cries 'Aha!' to the devil,
Like a mad lad,
125 Pare thy nails, dad.
Adieu, goodman devil.   *Exit*

Act 4 Scene 3   *running scene 16*

Enter Sebastian

SEBASTIAN   This is the air, that is the glorious sun,
This pearl she gave me, I do feel't and see't.   *Holds up a pearl*

---

104 Well-a-day alas/would   **113 requite** repay   **118 a trice** an instant   **119 Vice**
buffoon/comic character in old morality plays   **121 dagger of lath** the weapon of the Vice
character   **lath** thin wood   **125 Pare thy nails** probably a comic routine in morality plays
Pare trim   **dad** the Vice was sometimes portrayed as the devil's son   **126 goodman** title for
someone below the rank of gentleman

And though 'tis wonder that enwraps me thus,
Yet 'tis not madness. Where's Antonio, then?
5   I could not find him at the Elephant.
Yet there he was, and there I found this credit,
That he did range the town to seek me out.
His counsel now might do me golden service,
For though my soul disputes well with my sense
10   That this may be some error but no madness,
Yet doth this accident and flood of fortune
So far exceed all instance, all discourse,
That I am ready to distrust mine eyes
And wrangle with my reason that persuades me
15   To any other trust but that I am mad,
Or else the lady's mad; yet, if 'twere so,
She could not sway her house, command her followers,
Take and give back affairs and their dispatch
With such a smooth, discreet and stable bearing
20   As I perceive she does. There's something in't
That is deceivable. But here the lady comes.

Enter Olivia and Priest

OLIVIA   Blame not this haste of mine. If you mean well,
Now go with me and with this holy man
Into the chantry by: there, before him,
25   And underneath that consecrated roof,
Plight me the full assurance of your faith,
That my most jealous and too doubtful soul
May live at peace. He shall conceal it
Whiles you are willing it shall come to note,
30   What time we will our celebration keep
According to my birth. What do you say?

4.3   **6 was** had been   **credit** report   **7 range** roam   **9 disputes well** i.e. agrees
11 accident unforeseen event   **12 instance** precedent   **discourse** rationality   **14 wrangle**
argue   **15 trust** belief   **17 sway her house** govern her household   **18 Take . . . dispatch**
deal with matters of household business   **21 deceivable** deceptive   **24 chantry** private
chapel   **by** nearby   **26 Plight . . . faith** pledge your love (in a binding betrothal)   **27 jealous**
anxious, uncertain, wary   **29 Whiles** until   **note** public knowledge   **30 What** at which
celebration i.e. marriage   **31 birth** social status

SEBASTIAN   I'll follow this good man, and go with you,
And having sworn truth, ever will be true.

OLIVIA   Then lead the way, good father, and heavens so
shine,

35   That they may fairly note this act of mine!   *Exeunt*

Act 5 Scene 1   *running scene 17*

Enter Clown [Feste] and Fabian

FABIAN   Now, as thou lovest me, let me see his letter.

FESTE   Good Master Fabian, grant me another request.

FABIAN   Anything.

FESTE   Do not desire to see this letter.

5   FABIAN   This is to give a dog and in recompense desire my
dog again.

Enter Duke [Orsino], Viola, Curio and Lords

ORSINO   Belong you to the lady Olivia, friends?

FESTE   Ay, sir, we are some of her trappings.

ORSINO   I know thee well. How dost thou, my good fellow?

10   FESTE   Truly, sir, the better for my foes and the worse for my
friends.

ORSINO   Just the contrary, the better for thy friends.

FESTE   No, sir, the worse.

ORSINO   How can that be?

15   FESTE   Marry, sir, they praise me and make an ass of me.
Now my foes tell me plainly I am an ass: so that by my foes,
sir, I profit in the knowledge of myself, and by my friends I am
abused: so that, conclusions to be as kisses, if your four
negatives make your two affirmatives, why then, the worse
20   for my friends and the better for my foes.

ORSINO   Why, this is excellent.

---

35 fairly note observe with favor   **5.1   5 This . . . again** seemingly refers to the anecdote
about Elizabeth I and her kinsman Dr. Boleyn; she asked for his dog and promised him
anything in return, upon which he asked for the animal back   **8 trappings** ornaments/bits
and pieces   **10 for** because of   **18 abused** deceived   **so . . . affirmatives** if the outcome is
like the response to a request for a kiss, where "no, no, no, no" means "yes, yes"

FESTE   By my troth, sir, no, though it please you to be one of my friends.

ORSINO   Thou shalt not be the worse for me.   *Gives a coin*
25   There's gold.

FESTE   But that it would be double-dealing, sir, I would you could make it another.

ORSINO   O, you give me ill counsel.

FESTE   Put your grace in your pocket, sir, for this once, and
30   let your flesh and blood obey it.

ORSINO   Well, I will be so much a sinner to be   *Gives another*
a double-dealer. There's another.   *coin*

FESTE   *Primo, secundo, tertio,* is a good play, and the old saying is, the third pays for all. The triplex, sir, is a good
35   tripping measure, or the bells of Saint Bennet, sir, may put you in mind: one, two, three.

ORSINO   You can fool no more money out of me at this throw. If you will let your lady know I am here to speak with her, and bring her along with you, it may awake my bounty
40   further.

FESTE   Marry, sir, lullaby to your bounty till I come again. I go, sir. But I would not have you to think that my desire of having is the sin of covetousness. But as you say, sir, let your bounty take a nap, I will awake it anon.   *Exit*

Enter Antonio and Officers

45   **VIOLA**   Here comes the man, sir, that did rescue me.

ORSINO   That face of his I do remember well,
Yet, when I saw it last, it was besmeared
As black as Vulcan in the smoke of war.
A bawbling vessel was he captain of,

---

22 **though** even though   23 **friends** i.e. one who gives him **praise**   26 **But** except for the fact **double-dealing** duplicity/giving twice   29 **your grace** favor/virtue (plays on the customary way of addressing a duke)   **in your pocket** i.e. to hide it/to give money   30 **flesh and blood** human instincts/frailty   **it** i.e. the **ill counsel**   31 **to** as to   33 *Primo, secundo, tertio* "first, second, third" (Latin)   **play** game   34 **third . . . all** i.e. third time lucky (proverbial)   **triplex** triple time in music   35 **tripping** nimble, skipping   **measure** stately dance/music   **Saint Bennet** church of Saint Benedict   38 **throw** roll of the dice/occasion   41 **lullaby** i.e. farewell   48 **Vulcan** Roman god of fire, and the gods' blacksmith   49 **bawbling** trifling

50   For shallow draught and bulk unprizeable,
        With which such scathful grapple did he make
        With the most noble bottom of our fleet,
        That very envy and the tongue of loss
        Cried fame and honour on him. What's the matter?

55 FIRST OFFICER   Orsino, this is that Antonio
        That took the *Phoenix* and her fraught from Candy,
        And this is he that did the *Tiger* board
        When your young nephew Titus lost his leg;
        Here in the streets, desperate of shame and state,

60   In private brabble did we apprehend him.

    VIOLA   He did me kindness, sir, drew on my side,
        But in conclusion put strange speech upon me.
        I know not what 'twas but distraction.

    ORSINO   Notable pirate! Thou salt-water thief!

65   What foolish boldness brought thee to their mercies,
        Whom thou, in terms so bloody and so dear,
        Hast made thine enemies?

    ANTONIO   Orsino, noble sir,
        Be pleased that I shake off these names you give me.

70   Antonio never yet was thief or pirate,
        Though I confess, on base and ground enough,
        Orsino's enemy. A witchcraft drew me hither.
        That most ingrateful boy there by your side
        From the rude sea's enraged and foamy mouth

75   Did I redeem. A wreck past hope he was.
        His life I gave him and did thereto add
        My love, without retention or restraint,

---

50 For (trifling) because of   **draught** depth of water required to float the ship   **unprizeable**
of little value   **51 scathful** damaging   **grapple** close fighting, attempts to board another
ship   **52 bottom** ship (literally, ship's hull)   **53 very** even   **envy** malice, i.e. his enemies
loss defeat   **56 *Phoenix*** name of Illyrian ship   **fraught** cargo   **Candy** Candia, modern
Heraklion, a port in Crete   **57 *Tiger*** name of Illyrian ship   **59 desperate** disregarding
60 brabble brawl   **61 on my side** (his sword) in my defense   **62 put . . . me** spoke to me
strangely   **63 but distraction** if not madness   **64 Notable** notorious   **66 bloody**
bloodthirsty   **dear** grievous, severe   **69 Be . . . I** allow me to   **71 base** basis   **74 rude**
rough   **77 retention** reservation

All his in dedication. For his sake
Did I expose myself — pure for his love —
80   Into the danger of this adverse town,
Drew to defend him when he was beset,
Where being apprehended, his false cunning —
Not meaning to partake with me in danger —
Taught him to face me out of his acquaintance,
85   And grew a twenty years removèd thing
While one would wink, denied me mine own purse,
Which I had recommended to his use
Not half an hour before.

VIOLA   How can this be?

90 **ORSINO**   When came he to this town?

ANTONIO   Today, my lord. And for three months before,
No interim, not a minute's vacancy,
Both day and night did we keep company.

Enter Olivia and Attendants

ORSINO   Here comes the countess. Now heaven walks on
earth.
95   But for thee, fellow — fellow, thy words are madness.
Three months this youth hath tended upon me.
But more of that anon. Take him aside.

OLIVIA   What would my lord, but that he may not have,
Wherein Olivia may seem serviceable?
100 Cesario, you do not keep promise with me.

VIOLA   Madam?

ORSINO   Gracious Olivia—

OLIVIA   What do you say, Cesario? Good my lord—

VIOLA   My lord would speak, my duty hushes me.

---

78 All . . . dedication dedicated wholly to him   **79 pure** purely   **80 adverse** hostile   **84 face . . . acquaintance** deny he knew me   **85 grew . . . wink** in the space of a moment he behaved as if we had not seen each other for twenty years   **87 recommended** committed   **95 But for** as for   **98 but . . . have** except that which I refuse him, i.e. love   **103 lord** if addressed to Viola, "husband" (Viola uses the sense of "master")

105 OLIVIA   If it be aught to the old tune, my lord,
            It is as fat and fulsome to mine ear
            As howling after music.

    ORSINO   Still so cruel?

    OLIVIA   Still so constant, lord.

110 ORSINO   What, to perverseness? You uncivil lady,
            To whose ingrate and unauspicious altars
            My soul the faithfull'st offerings hath breathed out
            That e'er devotion tendered! What shall I do?

    OLIVIA   Even what it please my lord that shall become him.

115 ORSINO   Why should I not, had I the heart to do it,
            Like to th'Egyptian thief at point of death,
            Kill what I love? — a savage jealousy
            That sometimes savours nobly. But hear me this:
            Since you to non-regardance cast my faith,
120   And that I partly know the instrument
            That screws me from my true place in your favour,
            Live you the marble-breasted tyrant still.
            But this your minion, whom I know you love,
            And whom, by heaven I swear, I tender dearly,
125   Him will I tear out of that cruel eye,
            Where he sits crownèd in his master's spite.
            Come, boy, with me. My thoughts are ripe in mischief:
            I'll sacrifice the lamb that I do love,
            To spite a raven's heart within a dove.   *Starts to leave*

130 VIOLA   And I, most jocund, apt and willingly,
            To do you rest, a thousand deaths would die.   *Starts to leave*

    OLIVIA   Where goes Cesario?

---

105 aught anything   **106 fat** gross   **fulsome** distasteful, nauseating   **110 uncivil** uncivilized
111 ingrate ungrateful   **unauspicious** ill-omened, unpromising   **113 tendered** offered (may
play on "tender," i.e. loving, gentle)   **114 Even what** whatever/exactly what   **become** suit
116 Egyptian thief character from a Greek romance who tried to kill a captive he loved when
his own life was threatened   **118 savours nobly** has a taste of nobility   **119 non-regardance**
disrespect/lack of attention   **120 that** since   **121 screws** forces   **123 minion** favorite/
darling   **124 tender** care for/value   **126 in . . . spite** to the vexation of his master   **127 ripe
in mischief** ready to do harm   **130 jocund** cheerful   **apt** readily   **131 To . . . rest** in order to
give you ease

VIOLA   After him I love
More than I love these eyes, more than my life,
135   More, by all mores, than e'er I shall love wife.
If I do feign, you witnesses above
Punish my life for tainting of my love!

OLIVIA   Ay me, detested! How am I beguiled!

VIOLA   Who does beguile you? Who does do you wrong?

140   OLIVIA   Hast thou forgot thyself? Is it so long?
Call forth the holy father.   [*Exit an Attendant*]

ORSINO   Come, away!   *To Viola*

OLIVIA   Whither, my lord? Cesario, husband, stay.

ORSINO   Husband?

145   OLIVIA   Ay, husband. Can he that deny?

ORSINO   Her husband, sirrah?

VIOLA   No, my lord, not I.

OLIVIA   Alas, it is the baseness of thy fear
That makes thee strangle thy propriety
150   Fear not, Cesario, take thy fortunes up.
Be that thou know'st thou art, and then thou art
As great as that thou fear'st.

Enter Priest

O, welcome, father!
Father, I charge thee by thy reverence
155   Here to unfold, though lately we intended
To keep in darkness what occasion now
Reveals before 'tis ripe, what thou dost know
Hath newly passed between this youth and me.

PRIEST   A contract of eternal bond of love,
160   Confirmed by mutual joinder of your hands,
Attested by the holy close of lips,
Strengthened by interchangement of your rings,

---

135 **mores** such comparisons   137 **tainting of** discrediting   138 **beguiled** deceived
146 **sirrah** sir (contemptuous; used to an inferior)   148 **baseness** cowardice/lowly nature
149 **strangle** stifle   **propriety** real identity   151 **that** that which   152 **that thou fear'st** him
you fear, i.e. Orsino   155 **unfold** reveal   160 **joinder** joining   161 **close** meeting

And all the ceremony of this compact
Sealed in my function, by my testimony.
165 Since when, my watch hath told me, toward my grave
I have travelled but two hours.

ORSINO   O thou dissembling cub! What wilt thou be   *To Viola*
When time hath sowed a grizzle on thy case?
Or will not else thy craft so quickly grow
170 That thine own trip shall be thine overthrow?
Farewell, and take her; but direct thy feet
Where thou and I henceforth may never meet.

VIOLA   My lord, I do protest—

OLIVIA   O, do not swear!
175 Hold little faith, though thou hast too much fear.

Enter Sir Andrew   *His head bleeding*

SIR ANDREW   For the love of God, a surgeon! Send one presently
to Sir Toby.

OLIVIA   What's the matter?

SIR ANDREW   H'as broke my head across and has given Sir Toby
180 a bloody coxcomb too. For the love of God, your help! I had
rather than forty pound I were at home.

OLIVIA   Who has done this, Sir Andrew?

SIR ANDREW   The count's gentleman, one Cesario. We took him
for a coward, but he's the very devil incardinate.

185 ORSINO   My gentleman, Cesario?

SIR ANDREW   'Od's lifelings, here he is! You broke my head for
nothing, and that that I did, I was set on to do't by Sir Toby.

VIOLA   Why do you speak to me? I never hurt you.
You drew your sword upon me without cause,
190 But I bespake you fair, and hurt you not.

---

163 compact agreement   **164 Sealed . . . function** certified by my priestly authority
165 watch clock   **168 grizzle** sprinkling of gray hair   **case** (animal) skin   **169 craft**
cunning   **170 trip** wrestling move to throw opponent   **173 protest** declare/swear
175 Hold little faith keep some part of your promise   **176 presently** immediately   **179 H'as**
broke he has cut   **180 coxcomb** head (with suggestion of fool's cap resembling a cock's crest)
184 incardinate incarnate   **186 'Od's lifelings** by God's little lives (mild oath)

Enter Toby and Clown [Feste]   *Sir Toby wounded*

SIR ANDREW   If a bloody coxcomb be a hurt, you have hurt me. I
think you set nothing by a bloody coxcomb. Here comes Sir
Toby halting. You shall hear more. But if he had not been in
drink, he would have tickled you othergates than he did.

195 ORSINO   How now, gentleman? How is't with you?

SIR TOBY   That's all one: h'as hurt me, and there's th'end on't.
Sot, didst see Dick surgeon, sot?

FESTE   O, he's drunk, Sir Toby, an hour agone. His eyes
were set at eight i'th'morning.

200 SIR TOBY   Then he's a rogue, and a passy measures pavin. I
hate a drunken rogue.

OLIVIA   Away with him! Who hath made this havoc with
them?

SIR ANDREW   I'll help you, Sir Toby, because we'll be dressed
205 together.

SIR TOBY   Will you help? An ass-head and a coxcomb and a
knave, a thin-faced knave, a gull!

OLIVIA   Get him to bed, and let his hurt be looked to.

                    [*Exeunt Feste, Fabian, Sir Toby and Sir Andrew*]

Enter Sebastian

SEBASTIAN   I am sorry, madam, I have hurt your kinsman.
210 But, had it been the brother of my blood,
I must have done no less with wit and safety.
You throw a strange regard upon me, and by that
I do perceive it hath offended you.
Pardon me, sweet one, even for the vows
215 We made each other but so late ago.

---

192 **set nothing by** think nothing of   193 **halting** limping   **in drink** drunk   194 **tickled** i.e.
beaten   **othergates** in another way, i.e. differently   196 **all one** doesn't matter   **there's
th'end on't** that's all there is to it   197 **sot** idiot/drunkard   198 **agone** ago, past   199 **set**
glazed/fixed/closed (**eight i'th'morning** may suggest the manner in which the surgeon's eyes
were fixed, rolling back, like the sun high in the morning sky)   200 **passy measures pavin**
stately dance, i.e. slow   204 **be dressed** bandaged   206 **coxcomb** fool   207 **gull** dupe/fool
210 **brother . . . blood** my own brother   211 **with . . . safety** in reasonable self-protection
212 **strange regard** odd/distant look

ORSINO   One face, one voice, one habit, and two persons,
A natural perspective, that is and is not!

SEBASTIAN   Antonio, O my dear Antonio!
How have the hours racked and tortured me,
220   Since I have lost thee!

ANTONIO   Sebastian are you?

SEBASTIAN   Fear'st thou that, Antonio?

ANTONIO   How have you made division of yourself?
An apple cleft in two is not more twin
225   Than these two creatures. Which is Sebastian?

OLIVIA   Most wonderful!

SEBASTIAN   Do I stand there? I never had a brother,   *Sees Viola*
Nor can there be that deity in my nature
Of here and everywhere. I had a sister,
230   Whom the blind waves and surges have devoured.
Of charity, what kin are you to me?
What countryman? What name? What parentage?

VIOLA   Of Messaline. Sebastian was my father,
Such a Sebastian was my brother too,
235   So went he suited to his watery tomb.
If spirits can assume both form and suit
You come to fright us.

SEBASTIAN   A spirit I am indeed,
But am in that dimension grossly clad
240   Which from the womb I did participate.
Were you a woman, as the rest goes even,
I should my tears let fall upon your cheek,
And say 'Thrice-welcome, drownèd Viola!'

VIOLA   My father had a mole upon his brow.

245   SEBASTIAN   And so had mine.

---

216 habit clothing   **217 natural perspective** optical illusion produced by nature   **219 racked**
tormented   **222 Fear'st** doubt   **228 deity** godlike quality   **229 here and everywhere**
omnipresence   **230 blind** heedless   **231 Of charity** (tell me) out of kindness   **235 suited**
dressed   **236 form and suit** physical appearance and dress   **239 am . . . clad** my body is
clothed with the flesh   **240 participate** have in common with all humanity   **241 the . . .
even** everything else is in agreement

VIOLA   And died that day when Viola from her birth
Had numbered thirteen years.

SEBASTIAN   O, that record is lively in my soul!
He finished indeed his mortal act

250   That day that made my sister thirteen years.

VIOLA   If nothing lets to make us happy both
But this my masculine usurped attire,
Do not embrace me till each circumstance
Of place, time, fortune, do cohere and jump

255   That I am Viola — which to confirm,
I'll bring you to a captain in this town,
Where lie my maiden weeds, by whose gentle help
I was preserved to serve this noble count.
All the occurrence of my fortune since

260   Hath been between this lady and this lord.

SEBASTIAN   So comes it, lady, you have been mistook.   *To Olivia*
But nature to her bias drew in that.
You would have been contracted to a maid,
Nor are you therein, by my life, deceived,

265   You are betrothed both to a maid and man.

ORSINO   Be not amazed; right noble is his blood.—   *To Olivia*
If this be so, as yet the glass seems true,   *Aside?*
I shall have share in this most happy wreck.—
Boy, thou hast said to me a thousand times   *To Viola*

270   Thou never shouldst love woman like to me.

VIOLA   And all those sayings will I overswear;
And all those swearings keep as true in soul
As doth that orbèd continent the fire
That severs day from night.

275   ORSINO   Give me thy hand,
And let me see thee in thy woman's weeds.

---

248 **record** memory   **lively** vivid, alive   251 **lets** hinders   254 **jump** coincide   257 **weeds**
clothes   261 **mistook** mistaken   262 **to . . . drew** inclined in the right direction (bowling
metaphor)   263 **contracted** betrothed   267 **glass** mirror/lens of optical instrument
(perspective)   268 **happy** fortunate   270 **like to** as much as   271 **overswear** swear again
and again   273 **orbèd continent** spherical container, i.e. as the sun keeps

VIOLA   The captain that did bring me first on shore
          Hath my maid's garments. He upon some action
          Is now in durance, at Malvolio's suit,
280   A gentleman, and follower of my lady's.

OLIVIA   He shall enlarge him. Fetch Malvolio hither.
          And yet, alas, now I remember me,
          They say, poor gentleman, he's much distract.

Enter Clown [Feste] with a letter, and Fabian
          A most extracting frenzy of mine own
285   From my remembrance clearly banished his.
          How does he, sirrah?

FESTE   Truly, madam, he holds Beelzebub at the stave's end
          as well as a man in his case may do. H'as here writ a letter to
          you; I should have given't you today morning, but as a
290   madman's epistles are no gospels, so it skills not much when
          they are delivered.

OLIVIA   Open't, and read it.

FESTE   Look then to be well edified when the fool delivers
          the madman. 'By the lord, madam'—   *Reads*

295 OLIVIA   How now, art thou mad?

FESTE   No, madam, I do but read madness. An your
          ladyship will have it as it ought to be, you must allow *vox*.

OLIVIA   Prithee read i'thy right wits.

FESTE   So I do, madonna. But to read his right wits is to
300   read thus: therefore perpend, my princess, and give ear.

OLIVIA   Read it you, sirrah.   *To Fabian, who takes the letter*

FABIAN   *Reads*
          'By the lord, madam, you wrong me, and the world shall
          know it. Though you have put me into darkness and given

---

278 **action** legal charge   279 **in durance** imprisoned   281 **enlarge** release   282 **remember
me** remember   283 **distract** mad   284 **extracting** distracting   **frenzy** agitation/
madness   285 **From . . . his** drove him from my memory   287 **Beelzebub** the devil   **the
stave's end** at a distance   289 **today** i.e. this   290 **epistles** letters/New Testament letters
from the apostles   **gospels** truths/New Testament records of Christ's life and teaching
skills matters   291 **delivered** handed over   293 **delivers** speaks the words of   297 ***vox***
"voice" (Latin), i.e. the correct manner of delivery (Feste has obviously read the words in a
"mad" style)   299 **read** discern   **right wits** true state of mind   300 **perpend** consider

your drunken cousin rule over me, yet have I the benefit of
305   my senses as well as your ladyship. I have your own letter
that induced me to the semblance I put on; with the which I
doubt not but to do myself much right, or you much shame.
Think of me as you please. I leave my duty a little unthought
of and speak out of my injury.
310   The madly-used Malvolio.'

OLIVIA   Did he write this?

FESTE   Ay, madam.

ORSINO   This savours not much of distraction.

OLIVIA   See him delivered, Fabian, bring him hither.

[Exit Fabian]

315   My lord, so please you, these things further thought on,
To think me as well a sister as a wife,
One day shall crown th'alliance on't, so please you,
Here at my house and at my proper cost.

ORSINO   Madam, I am most apt t'embrace your offer.—

320   Your master quits you. And for your service done   *To Viola*
him,
So much against the mettle of your sex,
So far beneath your soft and tender breeding,
And since you called me master for so long,
Here is my hand. You shall from this time be
325   Your master's mistress.

OLIVIA   A sister! You are she.

Enter Malvolio [and Fabian]

ORSINO   Is this the madman?

OLIVIA   Ay, my lord, this same.—
How now, Malvolio?

330   MALVOLIO   Madam, you have done me wrong,
Notorious wrong.

---

306 semblance outward show   **the which** i.e. the letter   **308 duty** i.e. respectful behavior of
a steward   **309 out . . . injury** as a wronged party   **314 delivered** released   **315 so** may it
thought on considered   **316 as . . . wife** as good a sister-in-law as you'd hoped to regard me as
a wife   **317 th'alliance** the union (in a double wedding)   **318 proper** personal   **319 apt**
ready   **320 quits** releases (from service)   **321 mettle** natural disposition

OLIVIA   Have I, Malvolio? No.

MALVOLIO   Lady, you have. Pray you peruse that   *Hands her the*
letter.   *letter*

You must not now deny it is your hand.

335   Write from it, if you can, in hand or phrase,
Or say 'tis not your seal, not your invention.
You can say none of this. Well, grant it then,
And tell me, in the modesty of honour,
Why you have given me such clear lights of favour,

340   Bade me come smiling and cross-gartered to you,
To put on yellow stockings and to frown
Upon Sir Toby and the lighter people?
And, acting this in an obedient hope,
Why have you suffered me to be imprisoned,

345   Kept in a dark house, visited by the priest,
And made the most notorious geck and gull
That e'er invention played on? Tell me why.

OLIVIA   Alas, Malvolio, this is not my writing,
Though, I confess, much like the character,

350   But out of question 'tis Maria's hand.
And now I do bethink me, it was she
First told me thou wast mad; then cam'st in smiling,
And in such forms which here were presupposed
Upon thee in the letter. Prithee be content.

355   This practice hath most shrewdly passed upon thee,
But when we know the grounds and authors of it,
Thou shalt be both the plaintiff and the judge
Of thine own cause.

FABIAN   Good madam, hear me speak,

360   And let no quarrel nor no brawl to come

---

334 hand handwriting   **335 from it** differently   **336 invention** composition   **338 modesty of honour** name of all that is decent and honorable/restraint befitting your status   **339 lights** signals   **342 lighter** more frivolous/lesser   **343 acting** undertaking   **344 suffered** allowed   **346 geck** dupe/fool   **347 invention played on** trickery sported with   **349 character** style of writing   **350 out of** beyond   **352 cam'st** you came   **353 presupposed Upon** previously suggested to   **355 practice** plot/trick   **shrewdly** mischievously   **passed** been perpetrated

Taint the condition of this present hour,
Which I have wondered at. In hope it shall not,
Most freely I confess, myself and Toby
Set this device against Malvolio here,
365 Upon some stubborn and uncourteous parts
We had conceived against him. Maria writ
The letter at Sir Toby's great importance,
In recompense whereof he hath married her.
How with a sportful malice it was followed,
370 May rather pluck on laughter than revenge,
If that the injuries be justly weighed
That have on both sides passed.

OLIVIA   Alas, poor fool, how have they baffled thee!

FESTE   Why, 'Some are born great, some achieve greatness,
375 and some have greatness thrown upon them.' I was one, sir,
in this interlude; one Sir Topas, sir, but that's all one. 'By the
Lord, fool, I am not mad.' But do you remember? 'Madam,
why laugh you at such a barren rascal? An you smile not,
he's gagged.' And thus the whirligig of time brings in his
380 revenges.

MALVOLIO   I'll be revenged on the whole pack of you.

[Exit]

OLIVIA   He hath been most notoriously abused.

ORSINO   Pursue him and entreat him to a peace.
He hath not told us of the captain yet.
385 When that is known and golden time convents,
A solemn combination shall be made
Of our dear souls.— Meantime, sweet sister,
We will not part from hence.— Cesario, come —
For so you shall be, while you are a man.

---

361 condition (happy) circumstances   362 wondered marveled   365 Upon because of
uncourteous unfriendly/uncivil   parts qualities/actions   366 conceived against
imagined/discerned in   367 importance urging   369 sportful playful   followed followed
up/carried out   370 pluck on induce   371 If that If   373 baffled tricked/disgraced
376 interlude short play   379 whirligig spinning top/roundabout   385 golden auspicious
convents comes together/calls us   386 combination union   388 hence here, i.e. Olivia's
house

390   But when in other habits you are seen,
           Orsino's mistress and his fancy's queen.

                                          Exeunt [all, except Feste]

FESTE   *Sings*
             When that I was and a little tiny boy,
             With hey, ho, the wind and the rain,
             A foolish thing was but a toy,
395   For the rain it raineth every day.

             But when I came to man's estate,
             With hey, ho, etc.
             'Gainst knaves and thieves men shut their gate,
             For the rain, etc.

400   But when I came, alas! to wive,
             With hey, ho, etc.
             By swaggering could I never thrive,
             For the rain, etc.

             But when I came unto my beds,
405   With hey, ho, etc.
             With toss-pots still had drunken heads,
             For the rain, etc.

             A great while ago the world begun,
             With hey, ho, etc.
410   But that's all one, our play is done,
             And we'll strive to please you every day.   [*Exit*]

---

390 habits clothing   **391 fancy's** love's   **392 and a** a very   **394 foolish** trivial/silly (may play on the sense of "lewd")   **thing** may play on the sense of "penis"   **toy** trifle/useless/fun (may play on a sense of "penis")   **396 man's estate** manhood   **397 etc.** indicates repeat of chorus   **400 wive** marry   **402 swaggering** bullying/quarreling   **404 beds** drunk to bed/ old age   **406 With toss-pots** like other drunkards

TEXTUAL NOTES

F = First Folio text of 1623, the only authority for the play
F2 = a correction introduced in the Second Folio text of 1632
F3 = a correction introduced in the Third Folio text of 1663
Ed = a correction introduced by a later editor
SD = stage direction
SH = speech heading (i.e. speaker's name)

List of parts = Ed

1.1.1 SH ORSINO = Ed. F = *Duke*
1.2.15 Arion = Ed. F = Orion
1.3.88 curl by = Ed. F = coole my **90 me** = F2. F = we **does't** = Ed. F = dost
    120 set = Ed. F = sit **123 That's** = F3. F = That
1.5.4 SH FESTE = Ed. F = *Clo.* **156 SD *Viola*** = F2. F = *Violenta*
2.2.30 our = F2. F = O **31 made of** = Ed. F = made, if
2.3.2 *diluculo* *spelled Deliculo in* F **24 leman** = Ed. F = Lemon **122 a nay-**
    word = Ed. F = an ayword
2.4.56 Fly away, fly = Ed. F = Fye away, fie **91 I** = Ed. F = It
2.5.102 staniel = Ed. F = stallion **125 born** = Ed. F = become **126 achieve** =
    F2. F = atcheeues **154 dear** = F2. F = deero
3.1.7 king = F2. F = Kings **65 wise men** = Ed. F = wisemens
3.2.7 thee the = F3. F = the
3.4.23 SH OLIVIA = F2. F = *Mal* **64 tang** = F2. F = langer
4.2.67 sport to = Ed. F = sport
5.1.200 pavin = F2. F = panyn **409 With hey** = F2. F = *hey*

SCENE-BY-SCENE ANALYSIS

ACT 1 SCENE 1

The play opens with music, a significant motif associated particularly with poetic expressions of love such as Orsino's opening speech. He describes the moment when his "eyes did see Olivia first," introducing the themes of sight and perception. Valentine reports that Olivia refuses to hear Orsino's suit, as she is in seven years' mourning for her brother. She is "veilèd," "like a cloistress," introducing the motif of dress and associated themes of disguise, concealment, and identity. Orsino reasons that if Olivia feels so much for a brother, she will feel even more for a lover.

ACT 1 SCENE 2

Viola, shipwrecked on the shores of Illyria, fears that her brother has been drowned. The Captain reassures her and tells her about Orsino's love for Olivia and how Olivia "will admit no kind of suit." While acknowledging that appearances can deceive, as "nature with a beauteous wall / Doth oft close in pollution," Viola decides to trust the Captain. She asks him to help her disguise herself as a young man.

ACT 1 SCENE 3

Lines 1–92: Sir Toby Belch defends his intemperate behavior but Maria tells him he should "confine" himself "within the modest limits of order," introducing a recurrent image which involves either literal confinement in clothes or rooms, or more metaphorical confinements of manners and social roles. Sir Toby's punning on "confine" and Maria's responses set the comic tone for the exchanges among this set of characters, and reveal Maria's sharp wit. Maria scolds Sir Toby for his "quaffing and drinking" and for bringing Sir Andrew Aguecheek to the house to woo Olivia, as "he's a . . . fool." Sir Andrew arrives and instantly proves her point; his foolishness makes him a figure of fun throughout the play.

Lines 93–125: Sir Andrew announces that he intends to leave because Olivia refuses to see him and he believes she'll accept Orsino's suit. Sir Toby encourages him not to go, arguing that Olivia will not "match above her degree, neither in estate, years, nor wit," raising the question of social status. Sir Andrew agrees to stay "a month longer" and confesses how much he enjoys "masques and revels." Sir Toby encourages him to "caper," arguing that it is in their nature to do so being "born under Taurus," thus raising another theme—fate and the influence of the stars.

ACT 1 SCENE 4

Viola, now disguised as "Cesario," has become a favored page of Orsino, who singles him/her out to speak privately. In conventionally poetic language Orsino describes how he has "unclasped" the "book" of his "secret soul" to Cesario/Viola, and sends him/her to court Olivia on his behalf. Cesario argues that he will not be admitted, but Orsino is confident that his youth will aid him and gives an ironically sensual description of the boy which reinforces the complicated nature of gender and sexual attraction explored throughout the play. He describes Cesario as so young he is almost feminine, with "smooth and rubious" lips and a "small pipe" for a voice, adding that Cesario's "constellation" makes him right for the task. Although she agrees to go, Viola reveals in an aside another reason for her reluctance: she is in love with Orsino herself.

ACT 1 SCENE 5

Lines 1–155: Maria questions Feste about where he has been, saying that Olivia is displeased by his absence and will turn him away, but he refuses to say. Olivia arrives and Feste engages in "good fooling," using the riddles and wordplay of his trade to please her and prevent her from throwing him out. Despite his role as "clown," he is intelligent and perceptive: his fooling often contains reason and truth, as he says to Olivia "I wear not motley in my brain," a reminder of the difference between appearance and identity. He wins Olivia round by suggesting that she is foolish to mourn for a brother whose soul is in heaven. Olivia comments that Feste improves but Malvolio cannot understand why she "takes delight in such a barren rascal" and she accuses him of having "a distempered appetite." Maria reports that there is "a fair young man" at the gate wishing to speak to Olivia, who sends Malvolio with instructions that, if the youth is from Orsino, she is "sick, or not at home." Sir Toby comes in, drunk, and Olivia instructs Feste to look after him; he comments that "the fool shall look to the madman," one of many references to madness in the play, often as a parallel to love. Malvolio reports that the young man insists on speaking with Olivia, who relents but veils her face.

Lines 156–295: The encounter between the two women, one veiled and the other disguised, visually reinforces the themes of concealment and identity, as does Viola's claim that "I am not that I play." Viola, as Cesario, begins to deliver Orsino's speech, commenting on how "well penned" it is, thus emphasizing its contrived, conventional nature in comparison with her own passionate extemporized speeches later in the scene. She/he defeats Maria's attempts to throw her out and secures a private interview with Olivia, persuading her to show her face, praising her beauty but condemning her pride. She/he tells her that Orsino loves her "With groans that thunder love, with sighs of fire." Olivia acknowledges Orsino's good qualities: he is "virtuous," "noble," and "gracious," but she "cannot love him." Olivia becomes more interested in the messenger, questioning him about his parentage, and encouraging him to come again. After Cesario leaves, it becomes clear that Olivia has fallen in love with "him," creating a humorous situation of mistaken identity/gender and perhaps commenting on the shallow or arbitrary nature of romantic love. She sends Malvolio after the youth with a ring, pretending it was an unwanted gift from Orsino.

ACT 2 SCENE 1

Antonio has cared for Sebastian since rescuing him from "the breach of the sea," but Sebastian decides he must now leave and refuses to allow Antonio to accompany him because the "stars shine darkly" and are an evil influence over his fate. He reveals his true identity and talks of his twin sister, Viola, who he believes is drowned. He describes her, placing particular emphasis on the likeness between them, thus establishing the potential for further complications and confused identities. Sebastian intends to go to "Count Orsino's Court" and, despite having enemies there, Antonio decides to accompany him.

ACT 2 SCENE 2

Malvolio returns the ring to Cesario/Viola but she/he does not tell him the truth about it, realizing that Olivia has fallen in love with Cesario. She/he expresses sympathy, claiming that Olivia had "better love a dream," and reiterating the illusory nature of her present identity. She emphasizes the unnatural state of affairs by describing her female–male identity as a "poor monster" and summarizing the problem: as a man, her love for Orsino is hopeless, but as a woman, Olivia's love for her is "thriftless."

ACT 2 SCENE 3

Sir Toby and Sir Andrew are drinking late. Feste arrives and his quick-wittedness contrasts with Sir Andrew's genuine foolishness. Feste sings a wistful song that reflects some of the themes and events of the play. They begin singing a "catch" together when Maria interrupts to tell them to be quiet or Olivia will send Malvolio to turn them out. Sir Toby responds with raucous popular songs when Malvolio appears and rebukes them for being drunk and noisy. He pompously tells Sir Toby that despite being Olivia's kinsman he will be thrown out if he does not behave. Sir Toby reminds Malvolio he is only a steward. Feste leaves and Malvolio accuses Maria of encouraging them by allowing them alcohol. After he has gone, Sir Andrew threatens to fight a duel with him but Maria claims she has a better plan: Malvolio is "an affectioned ass" who aspires to high status and she will use this "vice" against him. She plans to drop in his way a letter she has forged in Olivia's handwriting that will convince him his mistress is in love with him.

ACT 2 SCENE 4

Orsino, still indulging in his unrequited love, calls for music from Feste, who spends his time in both households. Orsino discusses love with Cesario/Viola, in a conversation that is fraught with ambiguity and dramatic irony, as Viola is forced to discuss love as though she were a man. She/he acknowledges that she/he is in love when prompted, but cannot say with whom. The conversation is charged with erotic undertones, which again raises questions about gender, identity, and the nature of attraction. Feste sings a melancholy love song and Orsino orders Cesario to plead once more with Olivia on his behalf. When Cesario suggests that Orsino should accept that Olivia does not love him, as a woman would have to whom Orsino was unable to love, he declares that there is a difference between men's and women's love. "[N]o woman's sides," he claims, "Can bide the beating of so strong a passion." Cesario relates how his "father had a daughter loved a man," who concealed her love and, as a result, "pined" with a "green and yellow melancholy." When Orsino asks if she "died . . . of her love," he receives the ambiguous answer: "I am all the daughters of my father's house, / And all the brothers too."

ACT 2 SCENE 5

Sir Toby, Sir Andrew, and Fabian conceal themselves in a "box-tree" to watch Malvolio's response to the forged letter. Malvolio enters, imagining his future life as Count Malvolio, especially the power he would have over Sir Toby. The indignation of his concealed audience creates comedy, as does the dramatic irony of the situation. Malvolio finds the letter Maria has carefully prepared to trick him and recognizes "Olivia's" handwriting. He painstakingly and vainly deduces that it is for/about him and that Olivia is in love with him. The letter urges him to wear yellow stockings and cross-garters, to spurn Sir Toby, and to smile continually in Olivia's presence as a sign of his love, all of which he resolves to do as he exits. The others come forward and Maria arrives, explaining that Olivia hates yellow stockings and cross-garters and is in no mood to be smiled at constantly. They go to watch the effects of the plan.

ACT 3 SCENE 1

Cesario/Viola arrives and, after a quick-witted exchange with Feste, gives him money. Sir Andrew admires Cesario's courtly language toward Olivia, who orders all the others to leave. Cesario continues to plead for Orsino but Olivia confesses it is Cesario she loves. She/he responds with pity, swearing that "no woman" will ever be mistress of her heart.

ACT 3 SCENE 2

Sir Andrew is leaving since Olivia shows "more favors to the count's servingman" than she does to him. Fabian argues that Olivia intends to make him jealous and wake his "dormouse valour." He claims Sir Andrew has missed an opportunity, and Sir Toby, keen for him to stay so he can continue to spend his money, suggests challenging Cesario to a duel. He instructs Sir Andrew to write a letter with "gall enough in thy ink," emphasizing the difference between crafted words and reality. Maria calls them to have a look at Malvolio, who is obeying "every point of the letter."

ACT 3 SCENE 3

Antonio's strong attachment to Sebastian becomes more apparent as he addresses him in potentially homoerotic terms, expressing his "desire" and "willing love," furthering the play's exploration of the possibilities and complexities of same-gender love hinted at in Orsino's language to Cesario. Sebastian intends to explore Illyria but

Antonio cannot accompany him because of Orsino's enmity. Instead, he gives Sebastian his purse and arranges to meet him later at an inn.

ACT 3 SCENE 4

The fast pace of this scene emphasizes the confusion of the various deceptions that are under way.

Lines 1–76: Olivia muses how best to woo Cesario, then asks Maria to fetch Malvolio—such a "sad and civil" person will suit her mood. Maria replies that he seems to have gone mad and "does nothing but smile" but goes to call him. Olivia observes that she herself is mad, again drawing a parallel between love and madness. There is dramatic irony in the exchange between Olivia and Malvolio as he quotes lines from the letter he believes is from her. Olivia thinks he must be mad indeed and suggests he goes to bed, which he takes to be an invitation. Cesario's return is announced and Olivia leaves, instructing Maria to ask Sir Toby to look after Malvolio. Determined to read all events as evidence of Olivia's love, Malvolio recalls that the letter instructed him to "be opposite with a kinsman" and decides that she has called for Sir Toby as a test.

Lines 77–175: Sir Toby, Fabian, and Maria pretend to believe that Malvolio is mad and treat him accordingly until he exits in anger. They are delighted by the results of the plan and, in a moment of meta-theatrical awareness, Fabian declares that if he saw the scene "played upon a stage," he would "condemn it as an improbable fiction." Sir Toby decides they should lock Malvolio in a darkened room, a traditional treatment for madness. Sir Andrew arrives with his challenge to Cesario. Sir Toby reads it and Fabian pretends to approve while revealing the nonsensical nature of the letter and the foolishness of its writer. They encourage Sir Andrew to look for Cesario in the orchard. When he has gone, Sir Toby comments that the challenge will "breed no terror in the youth. He will find it comes from a clodpole," so instead of delivering it he will act as a go-between, inciting them against each other.

Lines 176–248: Olivia continues to woo Cesario/Viola, who displays a "heart of stone" and continues to plead for Orsino. When Olivia has gone, Sir Toby and Fabian accost Cesario and pretend that he has enraged Sir Andrew, who is waiting for him in the orchard, "bloody as the hunter." Bewildered, Cesario claims that he has no quarrel with anyone, but they pretend that he must have done something to upset him, describing Sir Andrew's fury and his history as "a devil in private brawl" who has killed three men. Alarmed, Cesario insists that he is no fighter and asks Sir Toby to speak to Sir Andrew on his behalf.

Lines 249–281: Sir Toby now describes Cesario's anger to Sir Andrew, who regrets challenging him. Sir Toby's aside reveals the pleasure he takes in making a fool of Sir Andrew. Fabian brings Cesario, and Sir Toby assures the two "rivals" that the other insists on fighting but has promised not to draw blood.

Lines 282–369: Antonio arrives and, mistaking Cesario for Sebastian, offers to fight on his behalf. Sir Toby draws his sword on Antonio but they are interrupted by the officers who arrest Antonio for his previous offenses against Orsino. Turning to Cesario, whom he takes to be Sebastian, he asks for his purse. Confused, Cesario denies all knowledge of it but offers Antonio half of his "coffer." Antonio is heartbroken by his friend's betrayal, claiming "Thou hast, good Sebastian, done good feature shame," before being taken off to prison. Viola realizes that Sebastian may still be alive and rushes off to find him, followed by Sir Andrew who thinks that Cesario is running away from the duel.

ACT 4 SCENE 1

Feste, believing Sebastian to be Cesario, is trying to get him to go to Olivia and becoming increasingly angry at Sebastian's claims not to know him. Sir Andrew arrives and, mistaking Sebastian for Cesario, strikes him. Sebastian retaliates and he and Sir Toby draw upon each other as Olivia enters. She orders Sir Toby to "hold" and "be gone," which he does, accompanied by Sir Andrew and Fabian. Olivia begs "dear Cesario" to "Be not offended" and asks him to accompany her back to the house to be told of Sir Toby's many faults and to learn to "smile at this." Sebastian questions whether he is "mad" or whether it is "a dream"—both repeated images of love in the play—as he willingly submits to Olivia's request.

ACT 4 SCENE 2

Maria helps Feste to disguise himself as "Sir Topas the curate" and he asks "what is 'that' but 'that' and 'is' but 'is'?"—an ironic question given that very little within the play "is" "that" which it seems to be. Sir Toby takes him to see Malvolio who is locked up. Malvolio begs the "priest" to believe he is not mad, but Feste toys cruelly with him: when Malvolio says that he is in "hideous darkness," Feste tells him that he is in a room full of windows and must be mad. Sir Toby then tells Feste to speak to Malvolio as himself to see if the joke might be ended without trouble as he fears Olivia's reaction. Feste then converses with Malvolio as himself and as "Sir Topas," increasing the confusion of his identity. He agrees to bring light, ink, and paper so that Malvolio can write to Olivia.

ACT 4 SCENE 3

Bewildered, Sebastian wonders whether he "Or else the lady's mad," as he contemplates Olivia's love for him. He wonders where Antonio is as he would like to discuss the situation with him, but when Olivia arrives with a priest he agrees to marry her.

ACT 5 SCENE 1

Lines 1–97: Fabian wants to read Malvolio's letter, but Feste refuses to let him. Orsino and Cesario ask for Olivia and Feste goes to fetch her. Antonio is brought in by the officers. Cesario tells Orsino that this is the man who rescued him from the duel and the officers explain that it is "that Antonio / That took the *Phoenix*." Orsino asks what foolish boldness has brought a "Notable pirate" to Illyria. Antonio claims that he "never yet was thief or pirate" and explains that he was drawn there by "witchcraft," enchanted by Sebastian, whom he believes to be standing next to Orsino. He calls Cesario a "most ingrateful boy" and accuses him of "false cunning." Orsino and Cesario are confused, explaining that Cesario has been in Illyria for the last three months.

Lines 98–152: Olivia arrives and demands to speak to Cesario, believing that she has just married him in secret. Orsino tries to woo her but she flatly rejects his suit and refuses to listen to any more of his wooing, claiming that it is as "fat and fulsome" to her ear "As howling after music." Stung, Orsino threatens to kill Cesario despite the fact that he, too, cares deeply for him. Cesario declares that he would die for Orsino because he loves him, at which point Olivia cries, "Cesario, husband, stay." Cesario denies any knowledge of their "marriage."

Lines 153–208: The priest arrives and, believing Cesario to be Sebastian, confirms that he is married to Olivia. As Cesario protests, Sir Andrew arrives calling for a surgeon as "the count's gentleman, one Cesario" has broken his head and "given Sir Toby a bloody cox-comb too." Cesario denies this as well and Sir Toby arrives, very drunk. As Olivia orders Sir Toby and Sir Andrew to be removed, Sebastian appears.

Lines 209–314: Sebastian, not seeing Viola, apologizes to Olivia for injuring her kinsman. Everyone is astonished by the likeness between Cesario and the newcomer, who is delighted to see Antonio. Finally, Sebastian notices Cesario and, astounded by their likeness, demands to know his name and parentage. After mutual question-ing, Viola reveals her true identity and Sebastian points out that Olivia "would have been contracted to a maid." Orsino reminds Viola of the number of times she has said that she loves him and asks to see her in her "woman's weeds," which are with the Captain, whom Malvolio has had arrested. Olivia still believes Malvolio to be mad but Fabian reads his letter and Orsino comments that it "savours not much of distraction." Olivia sends Fabian to fetch Malvolio.

Lines 315–411: Olivia and Orsino make peace and she offers to host the double wedding celebration at her house. He agrees and releases his "page" from service, saying that she is to become instead her "master's mistress," which reinforces the gender confusions of the play, particularly as he continues to call her "Cesario." Fabian brings Malvolio, who shows Olivia the letter and asks why she has treated him so badly. Olivia recognizes the writing as Maria's and Fabian confesses to the plot and explains the reasons behind it, adding that Sir Toby has married Maria as a reward for her wit. Malvolio swears to be revenged "on the whole pack of you," and although Orsino tells Fabian to entreat him to peace, this strikes a discordant note, as does the impossibility of a conclusion to Antonio's love for Sebastian, forgotten as everyone leaves for the "solemn combination" of their "dear souls," a symbol of the restored order. The play concludes with a wistful song from Feste.

TWELFTH NIGHT IN PERFORMANCE: THE RSC AND BEYOND

The best way to understand a Shakespeare play is to see it or ideally to participate in it. By examining a range of productions, we may gain a sense of the extraordinary variety of approaches and interpretations that are possible—a variety that gives Shakespeare his unique capacity to be reinvented and made "our contemporary" four centuries after his death.

We begin with a brief overview of the play's theatrical and cinematic life, offering historical perspectives on how it has been performed. We then analyze in more detail a series of productions staged over the last half-century by the Royal Shakespeare Company. The sense of dialogue between productions that can only occur when a company is dedicated to the revival and investigation of the Shakespeare canon over a long period, together with the uniquely comprehensive archival resource of promptbooks, program notes, reviews, and interviews held on behalf of the RSC at the Shakespeare Birthplace Trust in Stratford-upon-Avon, allows an "RSC stage history" to become a crucible in which the chemistry of the play can be explored.

Finally, we go to the horse's mouth. Modern theater is dominated by the figure of the director, who must hold together the whole play, whereas the actor must concentrate on his or her part. The director's viewpoint is therefore especially valuable. Shakespeare's plasticity is wonderfully revealed when we hear directors of highly successful productions answering the same questions in very different ways.

FOUR CENTURIES OF *TWELFTH NIGHT*: AN OVERVIEW

The first recorded performance of *Twelfth Night* was at London's Middle Temple on 2 February (Candlemas) 1602. The student barrister John Manningham noted:

At our feast we had a play called *Twelve Night, or What You Will*, much like *The Comedy of Errors* or *Menaechmi* in Plautus but most like and near to that in Italian called *Inganni*. A good practice in it to make the steward believe his lady widow was in love with him, by counterfeiting a letter as from his lady, in general terms telling him what she liked best in him, and prescribing his gesture in smiling, his apparel, etc., and then when he came to practise, making believe they took him to be mad.[1]

Despite Manningham's confusion over details, the play was certainly Shakespeare's *Twelfth Night* performed by the Lord Chamberlain's (later King's) Men, probably with Shakespeare himself among the cast. It is generally assumed that Robert Armin, the company clown known for his singing and musical abilities, would have played Feste, with the notoriously thin John Sincklo as Sir Andrew Aguecheek.

The play was probably written in 1601; it has been suggested that it may have been written for and first performed at court on Twelfth Night (6 January) 1601 before Elizabeth I and her guest, Virginio Orsino, Duke of Bracciano.[2] It was later performed before James I on Easter Monday 1618 and again at Candlemas in 1623, when it was simply called *Malvolio*. Charles I wrote this alternative title in his own Folio edition of Shakespeare's plays. The character's popularity is attested in Leonard Digges' 1640 commendatory verse to the first edition of Shakespeare's collected poems:

> . . . Let but Beatrice
> And Benedick be seen, lo, in a trice
> The Cockpit galleries, boxes, all are full
> To hear Malvolio, that cross-gartered gull.[3]

After the Restoration of the monarchy in 1660 and the reopening of the theaters, which were closed during the civil war and Interregnum (1642–60), Shakespeare's plays were divided up between the two licensed companies. Major innovations in performance style were introduced with movable scenery, creating a more visual, illusionist theater, and the presence of women onstage. *Twelfth Night* was assigned to William d'Avenant's Duke of York's Men. Shakespeare's comedies did not suit the taste of the new age though. Samuel Pepys saw three productions of *Twelfth Night* between 1661 and 1669, none of which he enjoyed, even though the leading actor of the age, Thomas Betterton, played Sir Toby Belch. Indeed, Pepys thought it "one of the weakest plays that ever I saw on the stage."[4] In 1703 William Burnaby produced *Love Betray'd, or, The Agreeable Disappointment*, an adaptation which retained only around sixty of Shakespeare's lines but failed in its attempt to update the play to suit contemporary tastes. "More radical transformations, such as William Wycherley's *The Plain Dealer* or Pierre Marivaux's *The False Servant*," which used Shakespeare's play as source material, were more successful.[5]

It was not until David Garrick's production at the Theatre Royal in 1741 with Charles Macklin as Malvolio, Hannah Pritchard as Viola, and Kitty Clive as Olivia that Shakespeare's *Twelfth Night* enjoyed popularity and success once more. Macklin's casting as Malvolio thrust the character into prominence, as the earliest productions had done. As with his Shylock in Shakespeare's *Merchant of Venice*, Macklin's psychological interpretation altered the perception of both characters, bringing out the pathos of the roles, making them more sympathetic, even "quasi-tragic figures."[6] This effect was subsequently intensified in Robert Bensley's performance in John Philip Kemble's production, of which Charles Lamb wrote, "I confess, that I never saw the catastrophe of this character, while Bensley played it, without a kind of tragic interest."[7] Kemble's 1811 production was the first to reverse the order of the first two scenes of the play—a strategy since adopted by numerous directors.

In the early nineteenth century emphasis was given to the play's musical and spectacular potential. Frederic Reynolds presented an operatic adaptation at Covent Garden in 1820 incorporating the masque from *The Tempest* as well as extracts from Shakespeare's sonnets and his narrative poem *Venus and Adonis*. At the same time, "breeches" roles such as Viola, in which women pretended to be men, with their transgressive potential for assuming figure-revealing masculine attire, became extremely popular. The American actress Charlotte Cushman, best known for her performance as Romeo to her sister's Juliet, played Viola in New York with her sister Susan as

Olivia. The production transferred to London's Haymarket Theatre in 1846. Samuel Phelps' productions at Sadler's Wells in 1847 and 1858 transformed Malvolio curiously into a Spanish Golden Age *hidalgo*, one nobly born but poor (Don Quixote is the most famous literary example of the type).

Charles Kean presented a typically lavish pictorial staging with his wife, Ellen Tree, as Viola in 1850. Five years later Kate Terry starred in Alfred Wigan's production at the St. James' Theatre in which, with some rearrangement of the text, she played both Viola and Sebastian. Kean's spectacular set was matched by Henry Irving's in 1884:

> The Lyceum Illyria is a land where ornate palaces with their cool balconies and colonnades and their mazy arabesque traceries, look forth among groves of palms, and plantains, and orange trees, and cedars, over halcyon seas dotted with bird-like feluccas and high-prowed fishing boats.[8]

While Ellen Terry was praised for her Viola, critics were divided by Irving's Malvolio. A number objected to his mannered delivery. "When an absence of humorous expression is required to give a speech its full comic effect, Mr Irving's restless eyebrows and obliquely twinkling eyes do him a disservice." The production's "tone of serious tragedy," which culminated in his collapsing into "a nerveless state of prostrate dejection . . . stretched on the straw of a dungeon worthy of *Fidelio*," was felt to unbalance the play: "There can be no doubt that the straw which clung to Mr Irving's dress from the mad-house scene was the last straw which broke the patience of a certain section of the first night audience."[9]

Augustin Daly's 1893 production, which featured a violent storm as well as a moonlit rose garden, cut and rearranged the text drastically. It was generally well received, though, both in New York and London when it transferred the following year. In the words of the critic William Archer, it had "the one supreme merit which, in a Shakespearean revival, covers a multitude of sins—it really 'revives' the play, makes it live again."[10] For George Bernard Shaw, Ada Rehan's Viola was the production's only redeeming feature: "the moment she strikes up the true Shakespearian music, and feels her way to her part altogether by her sense of that music, the play returns to life and all the magic is there."[11] Shaw deplored the liberties Daly had taken with the text, though, which included cutting the "dark-house" scene in Act 4 when Malvolio is imprisoned and taunted with madness.

Surprisingly, William Poel also cut this scene in his experimental production at the Middle Temple in 1897 in the (reconstructed) hall where Manningham had seen the Chamberlain's Men perform it. Keen to gauge its possibilities as a playing space, Poel's Elizabethan Stage Society employed original staging practices as far as possible. Herbert Beerbohm Tree cut the same scene in his production at the Haymarket in 1901. George Odell described it as

> the most extraordinary single setting I have ever beheld. It was the garden of Olivia, extending terrace by terrace to the extreme back of the stage, with very real grass, real fountains, paths and descending steps. I never saw anything approaching it for beauty and *vraisemblance*.[12]

Unfortunately the set's complexity made it impossible to strike so that a number of completely inappropriate scenes had to be played on it. Tree himself played Malvolio, emphasizing comedy rather than pathos as the "peacock-like" steward was always followed by "four smaller Malvolios in the production who aped the large one in dress and deportment."[13]

Essentially an ensemble piece with the lines distributed more-or-less evenly across the major roles, twentieth-century productions generally eschewed the earlier practice of building up a star part. Harley Granville-Barker's "legendary"[14] 1912 production at the Savoy Theatre, influenced by the ideas and practices of Poel, has proved of lasting significance in thinking about the play. Michael Billington records how

> Norman Wilkinson's black-and-silver setting, evoking a half-Italianised Elizabethan court, combined beauty with intimacy: there was a formal garden with a great staircase right and left,

with drop curtains and a small inner tapestry set for the carousal. The verse was spoken with lightness, speed, and dexterity . . . above all, Granville-Barker got rid of all the false accretions of stage tradition and sought for the essential truth of character.[15]

Lillah McCarthy's Viola was praised as was Arthur Whitby's Sir Toby. Henry Ainley played Malvolio as a "Puritan prig," while one of the chief innovations was the casting of the middle-aged Hayden Coffin as Feste, whom Barker saw as "not a young man," adding: "There runs through all he says and does that vein of irony through which we may so often mark one of life's self-acknowledged failures."[16]

Barker himself admired the French-language version by Jacques

1. Harley Granville-Barker production, Savoy Theatre, 1912, the "black and silver setting evoking a half Italianised Elizabethan court," depicting Henry Ainley as Malvolio, Arthur Whitby as Sir Toby, Leah Bateman Hunter as Maria, Hayden Coffin as Feste, and Leon Quartermaine as Sir Andrew.

Copeau first staged in 1914 at the Théâtre du Vieux-Colombier. He reviewed the 1921 revival favorably, noting with approval the "precision, variety, clarity and, above all, passion" of the actors' diction.[17] There were several revivals in the 1930s and 1940s. Edith Evans played Viola in Harcourt Williams' 1932 production at the Old Vic. Five years later, again at the Old Vic, Tyrone Guthrie directed Laurence Olivier as Sir Toby, Alec Guinness as Sir Andrew, and Marius Goring as Feste, with Jessica Tandy playing both Viola and Sebastian. Jacques Copeau's nephew, Michel Saint-Denis, staged the play at the Phoenix in 1938 with Peggy Ashcroft as a remarkable Viola, a production that was subsequently filmed for the BBC. In Margaret Webster's 1940–41 Theatre Guild production at New York's St. James' Theater the Jacobean masque provided inspiration for set and costumes. Helen Hayes' Viola was warmly praised, although opinions were divided about Maurice Evans' Malvolio, played as "a Cockney, a head butler raised to sublimation."[18]

Hugh Hunt's 1950 Old Vic revival owed much to the Italian *commedia dell'arte*—both "arty *and* hearty": "Its best bits are the hearty bits, centred around a fine scarlet-faced, broad-bottomed, big-bellied, rasping Roger Livesey as Sir Toby. Its worst bits are the arty framework which the producer has thought fit to provide."[19] Peggy Ashcroft playing Viola was singled out for praise:

It is long since I have seen a Viola so fitted to the play. Peggy Ashcroft is never brisk or pert, never self-consciously disguised . . . She is very quiet, very loyal. She does not juggle with words . . . this Viola realises what love can be—she is not toying with it—and the "willow cabin" speech comes from her with an absolute sincerity, with no kind of elaborate preparation . . . And this is not Peggy Ashcroft's finest moment: that comes at the very end, when Viola, her lost brother before her, answers his question, "What countryman? What name? What parentage?" with the barely-breathed "Of Messaline." Now the play is played. Viola has her reward at last in the strange bittersweet Illyrian world. The Old Vic can be happy indeed to have had such a performance as this at its opening.[20]

Sir John Gielgud's production at the Shakespeare Memorial Theatre in 1955 with Laurence Olivier as Malvolio, Vivien Leigh as Viola, Paul Daneman as Feste, Maxine Audley as Olivia, and Richard Burton as Sir Toby had been eagerly anticipated. Despite the beauty of the set and Elizabethan costumes and its star cast, Gielgud himself acknowledged that "Somehow the production did not work."[21] The critic Peter Fleming suggested: "There is a certain lack of heart about this elegant and well-paced production": Vivien Leigh's Viola, though "trim, pretty, poised and resourceful," had a quality of "non-involvement." Likewise, Olivier's "brilliant and deeply-considered study of Malvolio" possessed some "inner quality of reserve or detachment."[22] Billington concluded that "If one had to sum up his performance in a word it would be 'camp.' "[23]

Tyrone Guthrie's production at the Stratford Festival Ontario in 1957 was more successful in integrating the play's diverse elements. Siobhan McKenna's Viola won especial praise:

> With economical grace and shining eye she creates Illyria out of bare boards as divinely as if she had a vision of Heaven . . . With the security of Miss McKenna's power, Dr. Guthrie feels free to play his clowns as less silly than is the lamentable tradition. Sir Toby, Maria and Sir Andrew are well-defined characters.[24]

Against these,

> Feste became a sad, ageing fool full of the pathos of his position where he is retained not for his wit but for his length of service. His melancholy, honestly come by, thus makes Malvolio's even more priggish, rendering his gulling and final turning-off not only poignant, which it always is, but even credible which it seldom is.[25]

Critics were initially confused by Peter Hall's 1958 production at the Shakespeare Memorial Theatre, now regarded as a classic of its time. John Wain saw it as "a perfect example of how a Shakespeare play can be ripped apart by the twin steel claws of naturalism and gimmickry,"[26] while Alan Brien, having criticized every aspect of the production, concluded: "Mr Hall is wrong and I am right. And yet how I enjoyed every moment of his wrongness."[27] Peter Jackson offered a more positive assessment of its innovative qualities:

> What a rib-tickling, refreshing *Twelfth Night* Peter Hall has conjured up . . . a production that is smooth and gay and brimming with new ways to play old tricks. Dorothy Tutin's golden Viola is wonderfully boyish, breathless and bewildered and always completely audible. She is alive, and to be alive in a cast like this means working double overtime. To force Olivia to play for laughs while surrounded on all sides by comedians with far better lines does not give the actress a fighting chance, but Geraldine McEwan, with her piping voice and plaintive little gestures, draws such sympathy from the audience that the approach is almost justified.[28]

Designed by the painter Lila de Nobili and set in the Caroline court pre–civil war, the production was described by the critic Robert Speaight as "a rich symphony in russet."[29] It was revived two years later for the Royal Shakespeare Company with a substantially revised cast (discussed in detail below, along with other RSC productions).

One of the most successful non-RSC productions of the late twentieth century was at Stratford, Ontario, in 1975, directed by David Jones, with Kathleen Widdoes as Viola and Brian Bedford as a puritanical Malvolio. For his 1980 production at the Circle Repertory Theatre, New York, David Mamet allowed the actors to choose their own costumes in accordance with their conception of their character. This resulted in a medley of costumes which divided critics, many of whom thought it an "irresponsible gimmick," while others argued that it revealed "a fine intuition into the play's heart."[30] If critics were divided about costumes and several individual performances, they were unanimous in their praise for Lindsay Crouse's Viola.

In 1987 Kenneth Branagh directed the Renaissance Theatre Company's production at the Riverside Studios. It was set in a wintry landscape with a Christmas tree and a snowy cemetery. Richard

Briers' "first-rate" Malvolio was "nicely balanced by Anton Lesser's shaggy-locked Feste, Frances Barber's clear-spoken Viola, and Caroline Langrishe's Olivia."[31] The production was later re-created for television. In the same year Declan Donnellan's production for Cheek by Jowl played at the Donmar Warehouse after a lengthy provincial tour. It was a controversial and irreverent production, with the drunken revelers blasting out the Sinatra classic "My Way." Michael Ratcliffe in the *Observer* thought it "a *Twelfth Night* for those who had never seen the play before and those who thought they never wanted to see it again," whereas Peter Kemp in the *Independent* argued that "Self-indulgence—mocked in *Twelfth Night*—is pandered to in this production."[32]

Tim Supple's 1998 production at the Young Vic contrived to be both "visually simple, its costumes vaguely suggesting an Eastern exoticism, and aurally rich, the alien beauty of its Eastern melodies and instruments creating an Illyria of otherness and wonder."[33] For his final season in 2002–03 at the Donmar Warehouse, Sam Mendes staged the play in repertory with Chekhov's *Uncle Vanya*. With Simon Russell Beale as Malvolio, Emily Watson as Viola, and David Bradley as Aguecheek, it was "a production that found multiple dimensions of *Twelfth Night* with highly suggestive staging and music and a minimum of detail."[34]

Twelfth Night has been set everywhere and nowhere: in 2000 Shakespeare and Company set it "against fragments of a deteriorating seaside carnival"; in the same year the Theatre at Monmouth's production was set in "a 1920s seaside resort," while the Alabama Shakespeare Festival's production of that year created a "1930s cabaret mood." On the other hand, companies such as the "touring five-person troupe Actors From the London Stage, thrive on early modern practices such as open spaces and doubling, tripling, and quadrupling roles. In the 1994 performance . . . at the Clemson Shakespeare Festival, Geoffrey Church played Orsino, Feste, and Fabian."[35] Similarly, Shenandoah Shakespeare's productions in 1995 and 2000–01 successfully experimented with cross-gender cross-casting, with David McCallum playing both Maria and Sebastian. The 2002 all-male production at Shakespeare's Globe theater in London played with the sexual ambiguity of the casting, causing the audience to gasp as Orsino kissed Cesario. Mark Rylance found a great deal of unsuspected comedy in the part of Olivia, and Paul Chahidi was a wonderfully busy Maria. The production was especially successful when played in the hall of the Middle Temple, where Manningham had seen the original version exactly four hundred years before.

The play has continued in recent years to thrive onstage despite Michael Billington's contention that while "*Twelfth Night* may be Shakespeare's most perfect comedy, it is also one of the hardest to bring off in the theater because of its sheer kaleidoscopic range of moods."[36] The illusionist productions of the nineteenth century are a thing of the past, their place taken by film with all its potential for realism. There were a number of silent screen versions, including Charles Kent's for Vitagraph in 1910, which, despite lasting for only twelve minutes, employs relatively sophisticated cinematographic techniques.[37] In 1955 Yakov Fried produced a Russian-language version in black and white which critics have seen as a response to the death of Stalin in its "fresh air of political renewal" which "opens up Shakespeare's play into a world of expansive great houses and the rich, open landscape of faraway mountains, open fields, and the promise of unlimited vistas or reverberate hills."[38]

In 1937 the BBC broadcast a live excerpt of the play, the first known instance of a work of Shakespeare being performed on television, which featured a young Greer Garson. A 1939 television production of the entire play directed by Michel Saint-Denis starred Peggy Ashcroft as Viola and George Devine as Sir Toby. In 1970 John Dexter and John Sichel produced a version for television with Ralph Richardson as Sir Toby, Alec Guinness as Malvolio, and Tommy Steele as a youthful Feste, with Joan Plowright playing both Viola and Sebastian. Two years later Ron Wertheim's Playboy production was made: "As one might expect, the language of the play is ruthlessly cut to accommodate numerous and oddly innocent examples of Illyrian erotic revelry, rich in nudity, pastoral landscapes, soft-focus camerawork, and slow motion."[39] The BBC's 1980 version is generally regarded as more successful, "graced with spirited performances by Felicity Kendall as Viola and Sinead Cusack as Olivia," with Alec McCowen as Malvolio and Robert Hardy as Sir Toby.

It nevertheless "still suffered to some extent under the weight of canonical seriousness," and Ford notes: "There was a strange echo of the detailed, illusionistic settings of Beerbohm Tree."[40]

Trevor Nunn, who surprisingly had never directed the play on stage in his distinguished theatrical career, directed a successful film version in 1996. It was set in the nineteenth century and boasted a star-studded cast, with Imogen Stubbs as Viola, Helena Bonham-Carter as Olivia, Toby Stephens as Orsino, Mel Smith as Sir Toby, Richard E. Grant as Sir Andrew, Ben Kingsley as Feste, Imelda Staunton as Maria, and Nigel Hawthorne as Malvolio. The film opens by "inventing a kind of mock prologue that depicts the sinking of the ship and the rescue of Viola."[41] Ford argues that "Nunn's emphasis on song and music . . . allow his film to capture some of the aural energies of the play without compromising the film." Nunn successfully exploits filmic technique: "In one wonderful moment early in the film, Nunn uses the camera to capture the complex energies swirling within Viola. We see her in disguise, walking along the sea, determined to master her manly walk in a state of mind both resourceful and ironic."[42]

There were ironic references to *Twelfth Night* in John Madden's 1998 film *Shakespeare in Love* in which Gwyneth Paltrow played a young noblewoman called Viola who disguises herself as a boy in order to become an actor. In 2003 Tim Supple directed an updated version for television with Parminder Nagra as Viola, David Troughton as Sir Toby, Chiwetel Ejiofor as Orsino, and Michael Maloney as Malvolio. A Channel 4 documentary charted the course of production—*21st Century Bard: The Making of Twelfth Night*. In 2006 a contemporary teenage update called *She's the Man*, directed by Andy Fickman and starring Amanda Hynes, set the play in a prep school called Illyria.

AT THE RSC

Laughter in Illyria?

Twelfth Night is often referred to as Shakespeare's most melancholy or darkest comedy, and surely unrequited love and grief are not what you'd instantly think of as the basis for laughter. Nevertheless, the most painful of emotions are often the catalyst for the most beautiful of poetry. Writing about tragedy, Shelley believed, "The pleasure that is in sorrow is sweeter than the pleasure of pleasure itself."[43] Shakespeare's genius in *Twelfth Night* is to take the pleasure that we feel from tragedy and successfully combine it with farce to create a hauntingly bittersweet comedy. The effect on the audience is to have them on the verge of tears or laughter at any given moment. In doing so he has created the most potent mixture of pleasures derived from the light and dark sides of literature.

The director of a production of *Twelfth Night* has to make decisions about whether his or her production will attempt to balance the elements of light and dark in the play, or to go to one extreme or the other. Productions by the RSC demonstrate a wide variety of approaches, and the difficulty in succeeding with this emotionally complex play is shown in its reviews. Directors have invariably been criticized for omitting comedy, neglecting depth of emotion, or failing to find a balance between the two.

From the 1960s onward a definite shift took place in which the darker elements became the central focus—aspects such as the treatment of madness, sexuality, and the character of Feste were radically reexamined, altering the tone of the play:

> *Twelfth Night* is widely accepted as a supreme harmonizing of the romantic and the comic, sweet and the astringent. The admirable production, then, is held to be one which holds these elements in balance. It is in the inflection which a production gives to *Twelfth Night* that the special interest lies. And this inflection has undoubtedly modulated in recent years. Broadly, and crudely: *Twelfth Night* used to be funny, and is now much less so. What has happened?[44]

John Barton's 1969 staging is widely considered a landmark production because it was markedly different in tone from previous productions. His exploration of the psychological complexity of the characters created for one critic "the most austere *Twelfth Night* I have seen";[45] for another it was suffused with "a kind of wintry melancholy."[46] The program notes pointed to this darker reading:

> For some characters [Orsino, Viola, Olivia, and Sebastian] . . .
> holiday perpetuates itself . . . The other characters of the com-
> edy, by contrast, are exiled into reality. For most of them, holi-
> day is paid for in ways that have real life consequences . . .
> None of these characters can be absorbed into the harmony of
> the romantic plot. For the rest of us . . . the play is done and we
> return to normality along with Sir Toby, Aguecheek and
> Malvolio . . . we have been dismissed to a world beyond holi-
> day, where "the rain it raineth every day."[47]

Barton's production effectively used the sound of the sea to bring in
what Matthew Arnold in his great Victorian poem of loss, "Dover
Beach," called "the eternal note of sadness":

> The audience takes its seats to find Richard Pasco's Orsino lis-
> tening to his musicians. Presently an aural disturbance comes
> upon the music. It grows louder, and is identified as the sound
> of the sea crashing upon the shore.[48]

> Thus Orsino's longing for love is overlaid with the storm that
> heralds Viola's arrival, prompting, through the use of sound,
> the idea that she will awaken him from romantic delusion to
> reality and true love. The sound recurred during Viola's con-
> versation with Orsino in Act 2 scene 4 and during her reunion
> with Sebastian.[49]

Viola acts as a catalyst, a storm of honest emotion: "throughout the
play, the sea still tosses its waves: there are moments when the setting reminded me of the tunnel of a dream, a journeying place of the
mind."[50]

Critic Robert Speaight experienced a sense of "the howling of the
gale outside the gilded cage of Orsino's palace; reality at odds with
romanticism."[51] Even the comic characters were serious: "The
knightly revels are sad too. Barrie Ingham's Sir Andrew is a knight of
woeful countenance":[52]

Most startling and persuasive of the group is Elizabeth Spriggs,
Maria: no longer the usual bundle of fun, but a prim Edin-

burgh housekeeper in gold rimmed spectacles, besotted with Sir Toby and only mounting the Malvolio intrigue with the purpose of luring him into marriage . . . the essence of the reading appears after the carousel scene where she steals back hoping to catch Sir Toby alone, only to be packed off blubbering by the selfish old brute ("It is too late to go to bed") . . . Malvolio: the agent of so much fear in the household, and finally the most wounded member of all—broken double under the weight of his humiliation, [stumbled] off stage after handing Olivia his chain of office. It is not a happy household.[53]

In John Caird's 1983 production inherent melancholy resulted from the pain of love. The program, instead of the usual notes, was littered with Shakespeare's sonnets on unrequited and barren love: "Set in the Jacobean period, the production accentuated a sense of decay and confinement by employing a ruined garden, rusting gates, and a mortuary chapel as components of the set design."[54] Thunder rumbled in the background, only achieving downpour at the end of the play, cued by Feste's song. The impact of frustrated love and thoughts of mortality on Viola's psyche was demonstrated by an inspired bit of acting from Zoë Wanamaker:

the decisive moment in [her] performance as Viola came when reunited with Sebastian, she showed her deep fear that her drowned brother had returned as a ghost to frighten her. She had suffered enough already, and now, on top of everything, the spirit world was playing an unforgivable trick, trifling inexcusably with her deepest feelings of loss and grief.[55]

In recent years there has been a definite reaction against the "twentieth-century preoccupation with the play's melancholy."[56] Ian Judge's 1994 production played "the broad comedy to the hilt."[57] When discussing the play he observed that:

The beginning of *Twelfth Night* deals with bereavement: we see a girl hopelessly distressed, having lost her brother but then, because of hope and friendship she is able to re-invent herself: a disguise allows her to create a new life. That's comedy, not because it's funny, but because hope and joy can be seen to spring from happiness. *Twelfth Night* also shows the comedy of falling in love, which occurs when people turn themselves inside out and almost reach the edge of madness. There are a thousand different ways of laughing and I think that *Twelfth Night* touches them all.[58]

Taking a more extreme approach to the comic aspects, Adrian Noble's 1997 production had an exaggerated and comic nonrealist feel to the characters, setting, and costumes: "When there are gags to be gone for, Noble goes for them, adopting the anarchic visual humour of pantomime."[59] The set, with brash, bold primary colors, was reminiscent of a child's play-box:

> a pop-art playground complete with jokey lurid green carpet for the garden box-hedge. It's overhung by a day-glo blue arc, on top of which sits an orb that travels a day's length from west to east and sun to moon during the play's course.[60]

> The design . . . often seemed to take the 1950s (perhaps as perceived through *Carry On* films) as its historical cue . . . the production was, in short, bold, brash and cartoon-like.[61]

Michael Billington referred to it as "a kind of pop-art Alice in Illyria with little emotional reality or erotic tension."[62] Although entertaining, it annoyed critics with its gimmickries. Also, by playing up the comic aspects, Noble lost the poetry of the play. Dimension and depth were lost in the interpretation of the characters. The program notes reduced them to types found in an enneagram report,* and illustrated them with exaggerated and grotesque caricatures:

> *Twelfth Night* is the darkest and most haunting of Shakespeare's great comedies, its humour constantly shadowed by cruelty and a keen awareness of mortality. Here, however the

*Ancient personality test based on nine psycho-spiritual types.

poetry is almost entirely missing and you are left with little more than crude, one-dimensional farce.[63]

Noble's production was a reaction against the type of *Twelfth Night* that had emerged since the 1960s, a conscious lampooning of the Chekhovian take on the play which began with John Barton's production in 1969. The effect of treating the characters as purely comic creations, however, was revealing in the failure of these productions to make you *feel*. It appears that the comedy, inherent in Shakespeare's text, comes from the characters themselves and is most effective when actors play the characters straight. Judi Dench, who played Viola in 1969, remarked: "John Barton was the one who said it's such a bittersweet play, that if you do that [i.e. play it purely for comedy] it tips over. It's not pure comedy."[64] As academic and theater historian Ralph Berry explains,

a taste for dark comedy has long been prevalent . . . the entire network of assumptions sustaining the old *Twelfth Night* has collapsed. And that raises the whole question of what is called, for want of a better word, comedy . . . A modern production of *Twelfth Night* is obliged to redefine comedy, knowing always that its ultimate event is the destruction of a notably charmless bureaucrat.[65]

But, he goes on to ask, "Do we laugh at it?"

"Are All the People Mad?"

There is a great deal in *Twelfth Night* about madness . . . for all its comedy and charm, [it is] very much darker than that. Like so many of Shakespeare's plays, it's about what happens to individuals when their idea of themselves prevents them from taking in the reality of the world around them. They act irrationally, lose their sense of proportion, become—in a way—unbalanced.[66]

Orsino is a victim of a type of madness to which the most admirable characters are sometimes subject. Its usual causes are boredom, lack of physical love, and excessive imagination, and the victim is unaware that he is in love with love rather than with a person.[67]

Orsino's complete lack of reason with regard to Olivia's refusal of him has been emphasized in more recent years. Michael Boyd's 2005 production had him in various states of disarray and undress, in a half-waking, half-sleeping state, indulging his every "romantic" whim, at the expense of his personal musicians, who had to get up and play music whenever he dictated. At one point they appear in dressing gowns, obviously dragged out of bed to perpetuate his obsessive sickness. Clearly unbalanced at the start of the play, his fantasy became so overwhelming that, in the final scene, he threatened to murder both Olivia and Viola. The question of whether or not he had regained his sanity remained ambiguous.

This emphasis on the madness of Orsino's wooing threw light on the fact that his behavior and romantic posturing is as forced as that of Malvolio. Faced with Viola/Cesario, who expresses her true feelings for Orsino through her entreaties, Olivia is awoken by a genuine note of true love. One of the play's ironies is that the man who is most sure of himself and most grounded in reality, Malvolio, is the one who is treated as insane.

In 1987 Bill Alexander wanted to emphasize the "madness" of all the characters, and his set and lighting plots played an integral part in this:

> I wanted to stress in my production some of the links between love and madness . . . to show people behaving in ways that are extreme, or deluded, or uncharacteristic—slightly "touched" perhaps . . . I wanted a sense of the intense Mediterranean heat that can go to people's heads. So the stage set was rather like a Greek island—white-washed houses, bright blue skies . . . And the lighting was deliberately strong when people's behaviour was at its most illogical.[68]

The whitewashed walls of the set and the intense white lighting, specifically plotted for moments of "deranged" behavior, also encouraged a visual association with the white walls of a padded cell. This focus on madness was pursued to the end with a disturbing conclusion for Malvolio. Antony Sher, who played the part, "initially presented him as a figure of broad comedy, then showed the character degenerating through appalling suffering into real madness":[69]

[Malvolio] gives the impression of groping around in the darkness while his voice is amplified to suggest a hollow cellar . . . [he] is tied to a stake like a bear and he whirls round it like some mad animal. At the end of the scene, he presses Olivia's crumpled letter against his cheek, with a tormented, hallucinated look on his face. This is an extremely powerful scene, which suggests, in a pathetic way, that the borderline between the light abuses of festive misrule and real madness has now become an extremely thin one.

When Malvolio reappears on stage at the end, he is totally bedraggled and, red-eyed, tries to shield his sight from the recovered daylight. But after Feste has once more taunted him with the whirligig of time speech, Malvolio says the expected "I'll be revenged on the whole pack of you" in a curiously slow way that ends in a singsong. When he goes away, with a strange smile on his face, one understands that the joke has really been pushed too far and that he has become truly mad.[70]

Both this production and Michael Boyd's 2005 production made use of light inspired by the scenic device used in the play *Black Comedy* by Peter Shaffer, which takes place in the darkness:

instead of playing it in darkness, you actually put light on the stage. So what the audience sees are people behaving as though it were completely dark . . . Instead of dimming the whole stage, we would flood a certain area of it with dazzlingly bright light to delineate the dark room. Both Feste and Malvolio would have their eyes open. But it would be clear to the audience from the very first moment—by the way that they moved around the stage—that neither of them was able to see a thing.[71]

2. Bill Alexander production, 1987: Antony Sher as Malvolio, "tied to a stake like a bear . . . presses Olivia's crumpled letter against his cheek with a tormented, hallucinated look on his face."

[Michael Boyd] plays the dungeon scene in a blaze of light. Thus we don't strain to catch the sound of Malvolio's *de profundis*, but hear it and see it full-on as the rope-tethered Richard Cordery angrily prowls the stage like a captive wild animal.[72]

This being comedy rather than tragedy, the accusations of madness are usually uncovered before the characters are seriously injured, although we wonder just how far Maria and Sir Toby would have been willing to go in pursuing their "sport" to the upshot, without the self-serving interests that hold them back. Donald Sinden, who played Malvolio in 1969, believed that his degradation left him no option but suicide: "All his dignity has gone, everything he stood for has disintegrated, what is there left for him to do? Nothing . . . I saw it as a very tragic ending . . . Malvolio's a man without any sense of humor, and therefore, a tragic man."[73]

In Shakespeare's canon, the handling of Malvolio's torture is undoubtedly one of the most difficult scenes for a director to stage. The absurdity of the situation may have its own inherent humor, but it is a bitter and dark one, especially when we think of the usual Elizabethan treatment of the insane: in Romeo's words, "Shut up in prison, kept without food, whipped and tormented"; Rosalind, on the madness of love, mentions "a dark house and whip" as a cure. In Elizabethan times it was the general belief that mad people were mad because they were "possessed" by the devil or some evil spirit. An attempt was made by a priest or "conjuror" to exorcize the devil. If this failed, as it usually did, the poor unfortunate would be manacled and chained to the wall of a bare, dark cell, beaten or whipped to their senses. The cruelty of the prank on Malvolio can often elicit an uncomfortable response, and modern productions rarely let the audience off the hook. Do we laugh at it? That is a factor entirely dependent on the choices that the director makes.

"Nor Wit nor Reason Can My Passion Hide"

Gender confusion stands at the very heart of the amorous adventures and comic love-plots in the drama of the age of Shakespeare. The confusion starts from the fact that on the

Jacobean stage all the marriageable young women's parts in plays like *Twelfth Night* and *As You Like It* were written to be played by boys . . . Boys dressed as girls, girls dressed as boys, and (on stage) boys dressed as girls dressed as boys, all apparently add to the delicious pleasure of the erotic chase. Outside the close confines of marital love, family and reproduction, gender-bending is the name of the game—"as you like it," or "what you will."[74]

The influential Polish critic Jan Kott asserted that "Illyria is a country of erotic madness."[75] As evident as it may seem to a modern audience, this aspect had not been explored until the 1970s.

Peter Gill's sexually charged revival in 1974 was dominated by a large image of Narcissus—"a continuous reminder to the audience of the themes of ambiguous sexuality and erotic self-deception":[76]

All are intoxicated with their own reflections, and the function of Viola and Sebastian is to put them through an Ovidian obstacle course from which they learn to turn away from the mirror and form real attachments.[77]

There is nothing at all equivocal about the physical relationships. Orsino hugs Cesario to his breast with rapturous abandon: Antonio is plainly Sebastian's long time boy friend: and Viola all but tears her hair in anguish at Olivia's unfulfilled passion for her.[78]

Demonstrative physical contact pointed to the nature of the developing relationships. As Orsino sat listening to music, lounging on cushions, Viola/Cesario sat between his legs. On his asking Cesario if he had ever been in love, they playfully rolled around:

The Duke is young and lolls about panting and sighing, half-dressed, a sexy man, all male comradely affection with his courtiers, arms around them, head on shoulders on the huge Habitat cushions. And among them, Viola, small, white and utterly frozen as he fondles her/him while he talks about this

other love—frozen not just with horror but with tense, deliberately fraught repression.[79]

Jane Lapotaire played a very boyish Cesario. She said, "Viola takes
her boyhood very seriously—she has to in order to survive."[80] Olivia's
reaction to the reunion of Sebastian and Viola was comical. Wardle
described her as "licking her lips at the sight of the interchangeably
delicious twins": "her 'Most wonderful!' brought the house down. On
'Cesario, come!' Orsino caught the wrong twin. Olivia as she moved
away with Sebastian, looked back half wistfully at Viola, perhaps
wishing that it were after all possible to have both."[81]

It was not until 2001 that such an overtly sexual reading was
revisited: Lindsay Posner "cleverly locates his production in the
Edwardian age of uncertainty, when young feminists and suffra-
gettes were derided as unwomanly and dandyish male aesthetes
reckoned no better than effeminate":[82]

Orsino's caressing of Cesario's head as they listen to the "food
of love" seems far from blameless. When we first meet Sebas-

3. Peter Gill production, 1974: John Price as Orsino (right) lolling on cushions as Jane Lapotaire as Viola is "small, white and utterly frozen . . . not
just with horror but with tense, deliberately fraught repression."

tian, Viola's long-lost twin, he's getting himself together after
a romp on a large bed with Antonio . . . the butch black sailor
who's plucked him from the waves. Can this really be the
Sebastian who will resolve all by taking Cesario's place in
Olivia's bed and maybe even in her affections? As for Matilda
Ziegler's simpering Sloane of an Olivia, the kiss she plants on
Viola in the denouement suggests the root cause of her trouble was that her real taste had always been for laddish lasses
in uniform. Much of this is amusing enough . . . but the
rather tactless outing of sexual ambivalence undermines the
subtlety of Shakespeare's own games with the chemistry of
love.[83]

Zoë Waites and Matilda Ziegler decided that on the line "Love
sought is good, but given unsought is better" (3.1.157):

Olivia should kiss Viola . . . Lindsay's suggestion was that after
Olivia initiated the kiss, Viola, rather than pulling away
instantly, should respond for a brief moment. Lindsay's inten-
tion was to highlight the sexual ambiguity that reverberates
through the play . . . Although Viola's instinct might initially
be to pull away, the experience of such a loving kiss became
fleetingly seductive for her too. Brimful as she is with love for
Orsino, she is living with her own unexpressed erotic charge
and readiness, and the joy, or comfort, of sensual human contact is not to be underestimated![84]

The relationship between Antonio and Sebastian in recent times
has often been played as a sexual one. Director John Caird believes
that this is a vital misreading:

[Antonio] deserves gratitude, friendship, filial love—all the
most pure things. In other words, he has built Sebastian into
something of an idol, and that is one of the most powerful
forms of love there is. But if you make it sexual . . . then you
diminish the other much more important aspects of the play
that surround it.[85]

4. Lindsay Posner production, 2001: Ben Meyjes as Sebastian "getting himself together after a romp on a large bed with Antonio . . . the butch black sailor who's plucked him from the waves" (with Joseph Mydell as Antonio).

Conversely, Terry Hands believes that "It's a wonderful mirror to the Orsino–Cesario relationship . . . but also enables us to see doom very clearly in front of our eyes and to relate that to the other love stories in the play."[86]

Antonio sees things as they are, deals in the every-day realities of a relationship, while the lovers discover perhaps more heady and ambiguous truths by dalliance and impulse. Antonio is as much an outsider in his way as Feste and Malvolio are in theirs . . . The lovers swirl and exit, perhaps still wrongly paired, it matters not; but they leave Antonio stranded in front of the painted Narcissus, a baffled figure.[87]

It seems that in the last fifty years all possible sexual permutations have been explored. But does the overt imposing of a sexual reading on every character connected with the love plot provide maybe one dynamic too many? John Caird, who directed *Twelfth Night* for the RSC in 1983, pointed to what he felt was key about Viola's male/female persona:

Viola puts on men's clothes and behaves like a boy, she finds out what life is like in both camps, and by the end of the play she is more sexually complete than she was before. The male and the female have been married in her. Sebastian is going through a similar sort of journey. He is having a relationship of one sort or another with a man in which his masculinity is made passive.[88]

It is only on breaking the social conventions of their sex that the characters can meet on a spiritual level outside the affectations of courtly love. We see Orsino reverting to type when he refers to Viola as his "fancy's queen." The formulaic modes of communication which had been broken down by Viola's disguise appear to be reinstalled. Cesario, the catalyst of sexual turmoil, has gone, leaving behind him self-awareness—an understanding of both male and female aspects of the self, for all the lovers involved. As a Lord of Misrule he has been more successful than Feste.

"This Fellow Is Wise Enough to Play the Fool"

The Fool knows that the only true madness is to recognize the world as rational.[89]

Between the worlds of festivity and reality, self-delusion and sanity, sits Feste. He has been played variously as the orchestrator of the play's action, knowing commentator on the folly of the lovers, and even elevated "to an almost superhuman position."[90] This enigmatic character is "rarely played as genuinely funny."[91] The melancholic nature of his songs and his bitterly humorous remarks place him outside the "comic" plots, with the effect that in many productions the play is depicted from Feste's viewpoint. Prefiguring Shakespeare's Fool in *King Lear*, his witticisms attempt to awaken various characters to their "irrational" behavior, the affectations that keep them from reality: Olivia from her mourning, Orsino from his romantic delusions. Maria and Sir Toby use him to mock his true function when confronting Malvolio as "Sir Topas" with the converse aim of turning a sane but deluded man into a madman.

In an innovative reading of the part for Michael Boyd's 2005 production, Forbes Masson played Feste as an integral part of the play's action rather than the usual external observer. An extra dimension was given to the subplot by Feste's obviously hopeless love for Maria. The theme of unrequited love was extended to engulf his world and infiltrate his songs, with the effect that he is commenting as much on himself as on the Orsino–Viola–Olivia love triangle. After the interval we intruded on Feste alone at the piano playing a beautifully pained and sonorous melancholy song, the same he played for Orsino at the start of the play. On Viola's entry he started, as if caught betraying something of himself that he'd rather not show. Not the usual eager force in the plot to bring about the downfall of Malvolio, he walked off the stage in disgust at Maria's device, instantly seeing through her prank as a means to Sir Toby's bed. Painfully aware that he was losing her affection fast, Feste was kept dangling and manipulated by Maria with intimate touches and kisses. Reluctantly he plays the part of "Sir Topas," hoping that the trick will win her favor. One had the sense that Feste knew the inevitable upshot of the plot but, a victim of fate and his own affections, had to play out the game.

At the end of the play when Feste lamented that "the whirligig of time brings in his revenges," he intimated that the revenge was also

5. Forbes Masson as Feste in Michael Boyd's 2005 production: "After the interval we intruded on Feste alone at the piano playing a beautifully pained and sonorous melancholy song."

upon him. Maria had married and carried away the leglessly drunk Sir Toby, and he has incurred the displeasure of Olivia for his part in the deception of Malvolio. His final song was sung with anger and helpless frustration. Starting with a beautifully sung lament, the tone changed after the first verse and he angrily spat out the words "knaves and thieves" and "toss-pots still had drunken heads." Seeing him used and cast aside by Maria for a particularly vile and drunken Sir Toby, the audience were made painfully aware till the end that the clown who strives to please us every day suffers while we laugh:

> In his chequered suit and with every weary mark of distress writ large upon his whited face, Forbes Masson gives as affecting a performance as I can remember. He sings exceptionally well, accompanies himself on a pub piano and gets the balance between pain and redemptive levity exactly right. He perfectly captures the pathos of his rejection by Meg Fraser's cruelly teasing Maria before magnificently picking up his spirits with "I am gone, sir, and anon, sir."[92]

Nigel Hess, the composer for the 1994 Ian Judge production, pointed out that the songs contained in the play are hugely emotional and important and that the actor playing Feste has to be a skilled singer. "Every time Feste sings everybody on stage says, 'What a beautiful voice.' It has to be like that."[93] The difficulty of finding an actor talented enough to take on the role of Feste *and* sing has made this phenomenon a rarity. In 1969, though, Ron Pember, in a highly praised performance, "sang his songs with the gritty voice of the modern, unaccompanied folk-singer."[94] Probably the most vicious Feste on the RSC's stage, Pember brought in an element of class consciousness, which accounted for the bitter essence at the heart of the character:

> He was a working man among the leisured classes, deeply critical of their behaviour and bitterly dissatisfied with his own . . . [He] spoke like a Londoner, dressed like a faded Harlequin now reduced to busking, and hinted always at a radical's social distaste for the antics of privilege. He despised the

effeteness of Orsino's court, and his angry assumption that Viola considered him a beggar . . . had all the spikiness of class-pride . . . He was discomforting, an outsider, almost malevolently saturnine, defying the sentimental response to Malvolio's plight by pressing home his final accusations with heartless accuracy in Act V.[95]

The most effective, highly praised performances of Feste came from interpretations that focused on the more bitter, melancholic aspects of his character. Difficulties with the accessibility of his "jokes" have led to a conscious move away from Feste as "comic" fool to a focus on his more serious function within the play. At his most sublime, the pain he imparts to the audience derives from the fact that Feste sees the world too clearly. In every aspect of light he sees darkness, in every character of worth he sees a flaw. As a melancholy entertainer, a *corrupter of words*, aware of the follies of love and class, Feste can remind us of Shakespeare himself, who strives to please his audience regardless of the pain that they and he are subject to when the festivities are over, when the play has ended.

The critic Anne Barton believed that, from a modern perspective, this comedy with its great undertow of melancholy linked the two halves of Shakespeare's working life:

The play crowns, almost summarizes, the nine Elizabethan comedies he had already produced. Children separated at sea, a heroine forced to disguise herself as a boy, the wise fool, a girl who reluctantly woos her own rival in love, ill considered vows, confusion between twins: these are only a few of the themes which *Twelfth Night* picks up and elaborates from its predecessors. At the same time, this comedy prefigures the final romances.[96]

Twelfth Night was also written around the same time as *Hamlet*, with Shakespeare's other major tragedies, *Othello*, *King Lear*, and *Macbeth*, still ahead of him and, in its mixture of comedy and tragedy, foreshadows the so-called problem plays, *All's Well That Ends*

Well and *Measure for Measure*. As Janice Wardle points out, *Twelfth Night* is:

> One face, one voice, one habit, and two persons!
> A Natural Perspective, that is and is not.

Much of the play is light-hearted in character, with the comic potential of concealed and mistaken identities running rife. But the other "person" of the play is altogether less frivolous: many critics argue that the dominant mood of the play is sombre and dark, with its emphasis on self-deception and the transience of life and love.[97]

Illyria is a land which encompasses all the worlds that Shakespeare inhabits: "How curious a land is this—how full of untold story, of *tragedy and laughter*, and the rich legacy of human life; shadowed with a tragic past, and big with future promise!"[98]

THE DIRECTOR'S CUT: INTERVIEWS WITH SAM MENDES, DECLAN DONNELLAN, AND NEIL BARTLETT

Sam Mendes was born in 1965 and began directing classic drama both for the RSC and on the West End stage soon after his graduation from Cambridge University. In the 1990s, he was artistic director of the intimate Donmar Warehouse in London. His first movie, *American Beauty* (1999), won Oscars for both Best Picture and Best Director. His 1998 Donmar production of *Twelfth Night* (staged in repertoire with Chekhov's *Uncle Vanya* as his valedictory shows as the theater's artistic director), which he talks about here, featured Emily Watson as Viola, Helen McCrory as Olivia, and Simon Russell Beale as Malvolio.

Declan Donnellan is joint founder and artistic director of the highly successful theater company Cheek by Jowl, with the designer Nick Ormerod, his partner. Born in England of Irish parents in 1953, he grew up in London and read English and law at Cambridge University. He was called to the Bar at Middle Temple in 1978. For Cheek by Jowl he has directed many Shakespeare plays, including a hugely acclaimed all-male *As You Like It*. He has also directed for the RSC and the National Theatre, and has worked extensively in Russia, including a *Winter's Tale* for the Maly Drama Theatre of St. Petersburg. In 2000 he formed a company of actors in Moscow, under the auspices of the Chekhov Festival, whose productions include Pushkin's *Boris Godunov*, Chekhov's *Three Sisters*, and the *Twelfth Night* that he talks about here, which was brought to the RSC Complete Works Festival in 2007.

Neil Bartlett, born in 1958, is a director, performer, translator, and writer. He was an early member of the theater company Complicite, and has directed at the National Theatre, the Royal Court, the Goodman in Chicago, and the American Repertory Theater in Boston. From 1988 to 1998 he was a member of GLORIA, with whom he created thirteen original pieces including *Sarrasine* and *A Vision of Love Revealed in Sleep*; from 1994 to 2005 he was artistic director of the Lyric Hammersmith in London, where his thirty-one productions included stagings of Wilde, Maugham, Shaw, Rattigan, Stevenson, Dickens, Britten, Shakespeare, Molière, Marivaux, Balzac, Genet, and Kleist. He has written plays, acclaimed novels, and a book mediating gay experience through the figure of Oscar Wilde (*Who Was That Man*). His RSC productions include *Romeo and Juliet* and the gender-bending Edwardian-dress 2007 Courtyard Theatre *Twelfth Night* that he talks about here.

What does the title mean to you?

Mendes: It's a mystery to me. I can see why he chose not to call it "Malvolio" in the Folio, as it is so much larger than that, and I can see why he chose not to call it *What You Will*, as it sounds too much like *As You Like It*. But I think the title that he ended up with seems to promise a night of revelry, festivity, and disorder, and that of course is not what the play is. So I've always suspected it was a last-minute compromise!

Donnellan: *Twelfth Night*, for me, is a highly significant title. Twelfth Night, or 6 January, is the occasion for the Feast of Fools when masters and servants reversed status and played each other. But more significantly Twelfth Night is also the Feast of the Epiphany. A solemn feast of the Catholic church, it is the night of the Magi's visit to the Christ child. But the significance of the visit is immense, for it was the first moment when people in our world realized who Jesus actually was. His significance was understood. This moment of realization or revelation is central to Christian thinking, as it is the moment when the immanent is made manifest. The moment of human perception of the divine. Many writers, like James Joyce, were deeply concerned with this moment, and Shakespeare's plays are full of epiphanic revelations. For example, in many of the comedies, the heroine, filled with the spirit of active love, goes into disguise and her final unmasking is epiphanic. But we don't need to know the word "epiphany" to feel what it is. Falling in love can have the quality of epiphany, of understanding not so much a new thing, as suddenly and gloriously realizing what was always waiting there. When we feel "I love you" we may also feel "I will always love you," but when that love is very deep, we may also have the uncanny feeling "and I have always loved you!" When Viola and Sebastian recognize each other in mysterious images of time, change, and death, we are moved because it connects with our own sense of falling in love, with epiphany. On the other hand, the tragedy of Othello resides in his being unable to recognize this love in Desdemona.

Bartlett: The play is written under the sign of festivity, of license, of misbehavior. But it's not called "First Night"; this is the time when things go a bit too far, when people are at the end of their tether . . .

In Shakespeare's time, Illyria was a state on the Adriatic coast (Croatia today), but the name is also evocative of "illusion" and "lyric" ("If music be . . . ") and "Elysium": so should we think of it as a place of reality or of fantasy? And did your thinking along those lines shape you and your designer's choice of set, costumes, and temporal location?

Mendes: I didn't think of it as a place of reality at all. For me it was a place of illusion. The thing that came most to my mind when I was working on it was *Alice Through the Looking Glass*—Lewis Carroll's twisted logic, his peculiar brand of English melancholy. We even had

Viola step through a looking glass. I tried very hard right from the start to create a sense of it being a dreamscape. When Emily Watson, who played Viola, arrived in Illyria she was talking to a succession of mysterious figures in the shadows—one wasn't sure if she was awake or dreaming. And yet, rather like Lewis Carroll, once we entered this world, once we went down the rabbit hole, there were many things about it that reminded us of England, and of a specific social structure. When we took it to Brooklyn Academy of Music in New York, beyond the mirror was an enormous pool, almost like a lake, covered with floating candles. Candles were also suspended over the acting area in both directions. That was a nod to the candlelight by which the play might first have been performed, and also to the sense of Christmas time and of Twelfth Night itself, but that gave it an even more dreamlike feel. So our Illyria had a firmly nonnaturalistic framework holding within it something resembling a real world.

Donnellan: All of Shakespeare's plays take place first and foremost on a stage, and this space changes and articulates shifting worlds and different realities. For example, in the history plays Shakespeare is not putting the "real" medieval world on stage but creating another theatrical world. We cannot understand Shakespeare if we reduce him to an everyday naturalism or historical accuracy. If we get locked in the merciless logic of spatial or indeed psychological logic, we miss the point.

In *Twelfth Night* Shakespeare presents a number of different worlds. There is the world of Olivia's house, which is very different to Orsino's court; running between them is the dangerous space of the path that separates these masculine and feminine spaces. Danger hides on this path, but so does love. Pirates get arrested but rings are found.

For me as a director, "space" is the very first challenge to be investigated. Investigating the worlds of Shakespeare's plays is the first step in all our rehearsals.

Bartlett: I think you have to play for real, and let the fantastical take care of itself—at least you do when you are working in the Courtyard Theatre, where no one needs to be told they are in the world of theater and make-believe. There were certain specific realities I wanted to root the play in. It is a play about the strictly hierarchical, upstairs/downstairs life of two aristocratic country houses. It is a play in which homoeroticism has to be part of the cultural zeitgeist, so that neither Antonio's homosexuality nor Orsino's . . . confusion (!) need any great explanation. It is a play in which we have to take for granted that a single woman as intelligent and wealthy as Olivia can both dream of running her own life and yet absolutely be denied that possibility by her society—i.e. everyone expects that she should marry her neighbor now that her brother and father are both dead. A costume-drama version of the turn of the nineteenth century seemed to provide all the right clues . . . but apart from the costumes, the stage was bare—letting the words and the music and the laughs do the work.

In one obvious respect our production was "fantastical"—in order to provide more good roles for women than is normally possible in a Shakespeare company, I cast three actresses in three of the male roles, capitalizing on the fact that cross-dressing and sexual license and low comedy are all central to both the atmosphere and the mechanics of this particular play. If men can drag up on *Twelfth Night*, then surely women can too.

Social status is a big part of the comedy. Did that also affect the period and setting you chose for the play?

Mendes: Yes, the world of the play needs a hierarchy, especially in Olivia's household. So that of course did affect the settings and clothes. I feel you do need to sense that Sir Toby and Maria are somehow "below stairs" in the servants' quarters; you need a sense that Malvolio is a steward, that Fabian is a footman of some sort. Beyond that, the one character who I felt needed to be defined and clarified by costuming was Feste. My feeling with all Shakespearean fools is that they need to be firmly rooted in the world of the play; the moment they stand outside it and don the comedy checked suit and a little trilby your heart sinks. So for me, Feste was a tramp, a drifter; he's been in the household before, he's gone away for a while, he's moneyless, he travels with a knapsack and his guitar. It seemed to me to be very important that you get the sense of him as somebody who might be found on a street corner, with his cap in hand, begging for coins. He's obviously impoverished and he obviously needs to earn a crust. That was important, as it somewhat clarified his dislike of Malvolio.

And of course for Malvolio's downfall to work he needs to be established as a household steward. Then when he attempts to seduce Olivia, he is attempting to subvert the social order, to overturn the hierarchy of the household.

Donnellan: Our approach to the play and its period and setting is fluid throughout the rehearsal process; but of course no human beings have ever invented any world devoid of status or hierarchy (though many have died in the attempt!).

Bartlett: See my previous answer!

Shakespeare had boy–girl twins, who are never identical, but mistaken identity is at the heart of the play: how much of a factor is the "identical twin" question in casting Viola and Sebastian?

Mendes: I remember casting *Troilus and Cressida* at the RSC when Nick Hytner was also casting *King Lear*, and Nick said, "Oh, how much the twins look alike is the sort of thing that boring people talk about in the car on the way home!" Clearly you shouldn't cast two people who look wildly different, but whatever they look like, two good actors will move you in that final reconciliation scene come what may—it's a beautiful scene. Beyond that, dress them in the same clothes, the same hat, and if they're vaguely the same height that should be enough.

Donnellan: To a certain degree, and we would certainly avoid choosing actors who looked wildly different, but we also rely on the fact that the audience have both the desire and the capacity to suspend their disbelief!

Bartlett: Provided that one isn't a foot shorter than the other, the rest is acting—and pacing; if you stage the "near misses" of one scene moving into another right, then the audience does all the work of the doubling for you.

What does disguise—and playing at gender-bending in particular—do for Viola?

Donnellan: I think it's more important to ask what these elements do for us. The complexity of love and particularly the fragility of human desire and sexuality is so crafted by Shakespeare that most, if not all, of his plays leave us asking questions about ourselves. Certainly the ambivalence of sexuality as it is figured by Shakespeare in *Twelfth Night* transcends most modern reductions into gay and straight.

Bartlett: Initially, it allows her to maintain some privacy while she sorts herself out—then it allows her everything; to lie, to flirt, to be with men . . . to explore herself. She needs to do this, because she's a powerless girl: Olivia and Maria manage to do all of those things without cross-dressing, but they're older, and wiser—and desperate!

"Cesario, come—For so you shall be, while you are a man": whereas Rosalind in *As You Like It* and Portia in *The Merchant of Venice* return at the end in female garb, Viola remains in male. We're even told that the Captain who is looking after her women's clothes has been imprisoned at the behest of Malvolio. Is this just a technicality: there's no time for a quick change? Or does it go deeper?

Mendes: I don't think Shakespeare ever does something like that accidentally. I think it does run deeper. I think the sexual ambiguity, which he plays on the whole time, is something he wants to linger on at the end, and I think it makes it much more interesting. You could say that what fascinates Shakespeare most of all are the unfinished stories, Iago, Leontes, Jaques—and here, of course, Malvolio. "I'll be revenged on the whole pack of you" is the line that hangs over the end of the play even more than Viola's last moments, or "The Wind and the Rain."

Bartlett: Yes, it goes deeper—if Viola is played by a young man. Both Orsino and the audience (at least in our production) hugely enjoyed the fact that he is "really" getting off with a gorgeous boy at the curtain call. It explains such a lot about him, don't you think?

Orsino can sometimes seem a rather shallow courtly lover in the opening act, then he's offstage for a very long time before his return at the end: does this present peculiar problems for a director and an actor?

Mendes: Orsino's a much better part than people think. I don't think it does present a problem. Mark Strong was sensational in the role. I think he's lovesick: in other words he's in love with the exquisite pain of being in love—a love that is unrequited. So once you've established that he is actually hungry for that state, is trapped in it, and is almost unwilling to come out of it, I think it's a wonderful part. Very funny actually, and rather touching. So it didn't strike me as an issue.

Donnellan: It is structurally curious; rather like the absence of Posthumus through the middle of *Cymbeline*, but this is possibly explained by the fact that the actor playing Orsino may have been playing another part. Orsino may have doubled as Maria—in which case the actor playing Orsino would probably have been rather short!

Bartlett: If you think he's shallow in his first scene, then you definitely have a problem. If, however, you think he is a powerful portrait of a powerful man—handsome, charismatic, sexy, obsessed, passionate—with some of the most drop-dead lines in the (or any) play, then you're all set for a great evening. If you think obsessive behavior, sexual ambiguity, and laughable human folly are "shallow," then you shouldn't be directing *Twelfth Night* . . .

Are we meant to believe in the marriage between Sebastian and Olivia?

Mendes: Yes. I think the easy way out when you direct it is to ironize those things in the last acts of Shakespearean comedies. The really difficult thing to do, like at the end of *The Winter's Tale* when Camillo and Paulina suddenly pair off, is to make the audience believe it. You could say that the real challenge of the play is to make these impossible moments seem possible.

Donnellan: The triangle of Sebastian, Antonio, and Olivia is complex. Both Antonio and Olivia give Sebastian money, which you notice he never manages to refuse. Olivia herself has the line: "For youth is bought more oft than begged or borrowed," which is remarkable. Certainly Sebastian's conversion from Antonio's love-object to Olivia's is very fast. It's hard not to believe that this rapid change is not lubricated by cash. Even Orsino is impressed by Olivia's wealth!

However, who are we to judge? When Sebastian sees the new sun, he sees that it is glorious. Perhaps he is more sincere than he seems. Perhaps he has been transfigured by love, like his sister. We often forget that Sebastian also disguises himself as Roderigo at the beginning of the play. Why should he do this? He is a complex character and far removed from a two-dimensional juvenile lead.

Bartlett: Well . . . it's not going to last very long, is it? He's over the moon—she's rich, beautiful, and (best of all, if you're a horny teenager who rather enjoys people falling in love with him) she is sexually and emotionally impulsive. She, however, is humiliated, furious, trapped in a marriage even more ridiculous than the one she escaped from with Orsino. Hardly a recipe for success. On the other hand, he is a very handsome young man, and well educated, and so who knows . . .

Music seems particularly important in this play. What implications did that have for your production? And what about Feste's songs in particular?

Mendes: Huge. Music starts the play, and sets its tone. It's crucial. It seems to me that when songs are sung, unlike any other play in the canon with the possible exception of *As You Like It*, people simply sit and listen to them. "Come Away Death" and "O Mistress Mine," they sit and listen, and then at the end we the audience sit and listen to "The Wind and the Rain." They're very static songs: even at the beginning with "If music be the food of love, play on," Orsino sits and listens. The act of listening to music is actually pivotal, it's central to the play. The music itself, therefore, has to have an emotional resonance. I was really pleased with the music, which was written by George Stiles. It's one of the things that I remember most from the production.

Donnellan: Music is integral to all our work. We began rehearsals by investigating the space through music, thus music was always crucial to our investigation. Feste's songs are crucial as he is the paid entertainer, exactly akin to the actors onstage.

Bartlett: Music is in the heart of the play. It opens it and closes it. The music is incredibly interior—apart from the "catch" scene, all the music is about hidden emotion. The last song, for instance, is the exact opposite of the communal merrymaking that usually closed an Elizabethan comedy . . . that's why I put Feste and his grand piano in the center of the stage. For all its glorious mechanics, it's a very introspective play . . . it probes the heart, which is music's job.

At the beginning of the play Feste has returned after an unexplained absence. Did you and your actor feel it necessary to devise a "back-story" in order to get inside Feste's character?

Donnellan: Well, I have worked with five different Festes over the years and with each we discussed what might have happened previ-

6. Feste's songs are crucial "as he is the paid entertainer, exactly akin to the actors onstage": Igor Yasulovich as Feste and Dmitry Dyuzhev as Sir Andrew in Declan Donnellan's 2007 production during the RSC Complete Works Festival.

ously, his possible reasons for leaving the house, and each time I think we came up with different conclusions! But such work is crucial to give authority to the actor. Incidentally, most of these "discussions" would have taken the form of physical exercises.

Bartlett: Well, he's a musician, and a comedian, and they're always temperamental bastards . . . Olivia just kicked him out for a while, and he needed the work, so he's been moonlighting at Orsino's.

How did you stage the great letter scene?

Mendes: Once we decided to place it inside his bedroom it unlocked all sorts of interesting things. Because it was in his private space you immediately got drawn into his private fantasy world in a much more serious way. There was a sense that he did this all the time, that he had a very vivid fantasy world which involved him and Olivia on a regular basis. This wasn't new, it was something that he'd already been fantasizing about for years. He lay on his bed and was clearly about to indulge in a sexual fantasy, and there was a feeling that we shouldn't be in this room with him, and neither should Sir Toby, Andrew, and Fabian, who were hiding behind the screen.

Donnellan: We decided to take the character of Malvolio absolutely seriously. This made the pain and humiliation that Malvolio experiences all the more serious and real, which in turn made it all the more funny. Comedy always has its feet in pain!

Bartlett: It staged itself. We were working on a bare stage, and didn't need a box-tree because we already had a grand piano to hide behind, so it was just a question of working out, move by move, how three people could hide from a fourth on a bare stage as he shared his predicament with the audience . . . my only rule was that he could never stand still or face one way for very long—otherwise there's no gag, they're just safely upstage and he's safely downstage. The whole point is that the scene is a virtuoso demonstration of the fact that love is blind; even though they're right there with him, he never sees them. Of course it helps if your Malvolio (John Lithgow) is six foot three and a natural physical clown.

Sir Toby and Sir Andrew are often perceived as especially lovable characters, but Malvolio's view of them as idle drunken parasites is not without justice, is it?

Mendes: No, I think they're complete liggers! They're total leeches, especially Sir Toby. They live off other people, they don't do a stroke of work. But at the same time they're not entirely wrong when they seem to ask, "What's the point?" For me, the key to Sir Toby and Sir Andrew is that they're older characters, coming into the twilight of their lives, dealing with past disappointments, and learning to come to terms with compromise. They're not young and vivacious, they're drinking to stave off melancholy, and to forget. There's a tangible sense of disappointment about them and Toby's cruelty emerges out of that: his own self-loathing, his own sense of regret. However, it is Sir Toby who in many ways drives the action of the play, particularly in the second half.

Donnellan: No, I think there are things to be said for and against all of Shakespeare's characters. Shakespeare is anti-sentimental and he is great precisely because he is nonjudgmental about his characters. Like Chekhov, Shakespeare invites us to draw our own conclusions about the characters he presents.

Bartlett: Some of my best friends are idle, drunken parasites. What's your point?

Is the gulling of Malvolio taken too far, when it comes to the darkened room? And does he recover his dignity at the end of the play? Whether or not his final exit line ("I'll be revenged . . . ") gets a laugh—or what kind of laugh it gets—is often the test of a production.

Mendes: Too far compared to what? It's taken as far as it needs to be taken in order to articulate the darkness in the story. I pushed it as far as I possibly could without distorting it. I think it tips over into cruelty, yes. I think that there is a streak of cruelty in Feste. He taunts Malvolio beyond what might seem funny or humane. I love those moments when darkness enters the comedies, they are the most exciting for me. Does Malvolio recover his dignity? Well, he recovers his seriousness: whether he recovers his dignity is in a way up to the director and the actor. You can have him recover his seriousness then have him walk off with his clothes flapping around his heels and he's funny. I didn't want him to make him funny. I wanted to make him frightening.

I didn't go into this production with a set of preconceived ideas or a heavily conceptual framework. I went into it with an open mind, and it was very unformed, image-based ideas that seemed to lead me. The only idea I presented to Simon Russell Beale [Malvolio] at the beginning of the process was to wonder how it would be if we were given access to Malvolio's inner space. So the letter scene, which normally happens in the garden, happened in his bedroom, and the box-tree was actually a screen with a print of a box-tree on it. That unlocked a lot of different things in the role. One felt one had been shown inside Malvolio's inner sanctum, and that made him seem very vulnerable. So his punishment consequently felt all the more harsh. And in part because of that, I think, the line "I'll be

7. Simon Russell Beale as Malvolio in Sam Mendes' 2002 production at the Donmar Warehouse in London—the letter scene set in a bedroom ("the box-tree was actually a screen with a print of a box-tree on it. That unlocked a lot of different things in the role").

8. The humiliation of Malvolio goes "way too far. So does the humiliation of Olivia when she realizes she's married the wrong teenager": Jason Merrells as Orsino, Chris New as Viola, and Justine Mitchell as Olivia in Neil Bartlett's 2007 production in the Courtyard Theatre, Stratford-upon-Avon.

revenged . . ." was met with silence. Dead silence. It wasn't funny, it was awkward. Like someone letting off an air-raid siren in the middle of a violin concerto.

Donnellan: We had a very special way of treating the exit of Malvolio. But you need to see the Russians do it! Anyway, how far is "too far"? There are many darknesses in the play that are unsuitable to lightweight comedy, but I don't know who could argue that *Twelfth Night* was merely a lightweight comedy.

The final grimness of *Twelfth Night* Shakespeare never lived to see. Thirty years later Malvolio came back, disguised as Oliver Cromwell, and was indeed revenged upon the whole pack of them. The puritans closed down the theaters and destroyed forever the particular form of performance that created the greatest plays ever written. But be careful, he still returns from time to time . . .

Bartlett: Yes it goes too far, way too far. So does the humiliation of Olivia in front of everybody when it turns out she's married the

wrong teenager. So does the humiliation of Orsino when Olivia publicly spurns his final offer of marriage. So does the humiliation of
Antonio when "Sebastian" denies him in public. And so on. I never
want to tell an audience if a moment is tragic or comic. Some people
find Malvolio's exit full of dignity and pathos. Some people think he's
a deluded, jumped-up, dirty-minded old idiot who's got his comeuppance, and laugh in his face. That's called live theater.

SHAKESPEARE'S CAREER IN THE THEATER

BEGINNINGS

William Shakespeare was an extraordinarily intelligent man who was born and died in an ordinary market town in the English Midlands. He lived an uneventful life in an eventful age. Born in April 1564, he was the eldest son of John Shakespeare, a glove-maker who was prominent on the town council until he fell into financial difficulties. Young William was educated at the local grammar in Stratford-upon-Avon, Warwickshire, where he gained a thorough grounding in the Latin language, the art of rhetoric, and classical poetry. He married Ann Hathaway and had three children (Susanna, then the twins Hamnet and Judith) before his twenty-first birthday: an exceptionally young age for the period. We do not know how he supported his family in the mid-1580s.

Like many clever country boys, he moved to the city in order to make his way in the world. Like many creative people, he found a career in the entertainment business. Public playhouses and professional full-time acting companies reliant on the market for their income were born in Shakespeare's childhood. When he arrived in London as a man, sometime in the late 1580s, a new phenomenon was in the making: the actor who is so successful that he becomes a "star." The word did not exist in its modern sense, but the pattern is recognizable: audiences went to the theater not so much to see a particular show as to witness the comedian Richard Tarlton or the dramatic actor Edward Alleyn.

Shakespeare was an actor before he was a writer. It appears not to have been long before he realized that he was never going to grow into a great comedian like Tarlton or a great tragedian like Alleyn. Instead, he found a role within his company as the man who patched up old plays, breathing new life, new dramatic twists, into tired repertory pieces. He paid close attention to the work of the university-educated dramatists who were writing history plays and tragedies for the public stage in a style more ambitious, sweeping, and poetically grand than anything that had been seen before. But he may also have noted that what his friend and rival Ben Jonson would call "Marlowe's mighty line" sometimes faltered in the mode of comedy. Going to university, as Christopher Marlowe did, was all well and good for honing the arts of rhetorical elaboration and classical allusion, but it could lead to a loss of the common touch. To stay close to a large segment of the potential audience for public theater, it was necessary to write for clowns as well as kings and to intersperse the flights of poetry with the humor of the tavern, the privy, and the brothel: Shakespeare was the first to establish himself early in his career as an equal master of tragedy, comedy, and history. He realized that theater could be the medium to make the national past available to a wider audience than the elite who could afford to read large history books: his signature early works include not only the classical tragedy *Titus Andronicus* but also the sequence of English historical plays on the Wars of the Roses.

He also invented a new role for himself, that of in-house company dramatist. Where his peers and predecessors had to sell their plays to the theater managers on a poorly paid piecework basis, Shakespeare took a percentage of the box-office income. The Lord Chamberlain's Men constituted themselves in 1594 as a joint stock company, with the profits being distributed among the core actors who had invested as sharers. Shakespeare acted himself—he appears in the cast lists of some of Ben Jonson's plays as well as the list of actors' names at the beginning of his own collected works—but his principal duty was to write two or three plays a year for the company. By holding shares, he was effectively earning himself a royalty on his work, something no author had ever done before in England. When the Lord Chamberlain's Men collected their fee for performance at court in the Christmas season of 1594, three of them went along to the Treasurer of the Chamber: not just Richard Burbage the tragedian and Will Kempe the clown, but also Shakespeare the scriptwriter. That was something new.

The next four years were the golden period in Shakespeare's career, though overshadowed by the death of his only son, Hamnet, aged eleven, in 1596. In his early thirties and in full command of both his poetic and his theatrical medium, he perfected his art of comedy, while also developing his tragic and historical writing in new ways. In 1598, Francis Meres, a Cambridge University graduate with his finger on the pulse of the London literary world, praised Shakespeare for his excellence across the genres:

> As Plautus and Seneca are accounted the best for comedy and tragedy among the Latins, so Shakespeare among the English is the most excellent in both kinds for the stage; for comedy, witness his *Gentlemen of Verona*, his *Errors*, his *Love Labours Lost*, his *Love Labours Won*, his *Midsummer Night Dream* and his *Merchant of Venice*: for tragedy his *Richard the 2*, *Richard the 3*, *Henry the 4*, *King John*, *Titus Andronicus* and his *Romeo and Juliet*.

For Meres, as for the many writers who praised the "honey-flowing vein" of *Venus and Adonis* and *Lucrece*, narrative poems written when the theaters were closed due to plague in 1593–94, Shakespeare was marked above all by his linguistic skill, by the gift of turning elegant poetic phrases.

PLAYHOUSES

Elizabethan playhouses were "thrust" or "one-room" theaters. To understand Shakespeare's original theatrical life, we have to forget about the indoor theater of later times, with its proscenium arch and curtain that would be opened at the beginning and closed at the end of each act. In the proscenium arch theater, stage and auditorium are effectively two separate rooms: the audience looks from one world into another as if through the imaginary "fourth wall" framed by the proscenium. The picture-frame stage, together with the elaborate scenic effects and backdrops beyond it, created the illusion of a self-contained world—especially once nineteenth-century developments in the control of artificial lighting meant that the auditorium could be darkened and the spectators made to focus on the lighted stage. Shakespeare, by contrast, wrote for a bare platform stage with a standing audience gathered around it in a courtyard in full daylight. The audience were always conscious of themselves and their fellow spectators, and they shared the same "room" as the actors. A sense of immediate presence and the creation of rapport with the audience were all-important. The actor could not afford to imagine he was in a closed world, with silent witnesses dutifully observing him from the darkness.

Shakespeare's theatrical career began at the Rose Theatre in Southwark. The stage was wide and shallow, trapezoid in shape, like a lozenge. This design had a great deal of potential for the theatrical equivalent of cinematic split-screen effects, whereby one group of characters would enter at the door at one end of the tiring-house wall at the back of the stage and another group through the door at the other end, thus creating two rival tableaux. Many of the battle-heavy and faction-filled plays that premiered at the Rose have scenes of just this sort.

At the rear of the Rose stage there were three capacious exits, each over ten feet wide. Unfortunately, the very limited excavation of a fragmentary portion of the original Globe site, in 1989, revealed nothing about the stage. The first Globe was built in 1599 with similar proportions to those of another theater, the Fortune, albeit that the former was polygonal and looked circular, whereas the latter was rectangular. The building contract for the Fortune survives and allows us to infer that the stage of the Globe was probably substantially wider than it was deep (perhaps forty-three feet wide and twenty-seven feet deep). It may well have been tapered at the front, like that of the Rose.

The capacity of the Globe was said to have been enormous, perhaps in excess of three thousand. It has been conjectured that about eight hundred people may have stood in the yard, with two thousand or more in the three layers of covered galleries. The other "public" playhouses were also of large capacity, whereas the indoor Blackfriars theater that Shakespeare's company began using in 1608—the former refectory of a monastery—had overall internal dimensions of a mere forty-six by sixty feet. It would have made for a much more intimate theatrical experience and had a much smaller capacity, probably of about six hundred people. Since they paid at least sixpence a head, the Blackfriars attracted a more select or "private" audience. The atmosphere would have been closer to that of an indoor performance before the court in the Whitehall Palace or at Richmond. That Shakespeare always wrote for indoor production at court as well as outdoor performance in the public theater should make us cautious about inferring, as some scholars have, that the opportunity provided by the intimacy of the Blackfriars led to a significant change toward a "chamber" style in his last plays—which, besides, were performed at both the Globe and the Blackfriars. After the occupation of the Blackfriars a five-act structure seems to have become more important to Shakespeare. That was because of artificial lighting: there were musical interludes between the acts, while the candles were trimmed and replaced. Again, though, something similar must have been necessary for indoor court performances throughout his career.

Front of house there were the "gatherers" who collected the money from audience members: a penny to stand in the open-air yard, another penny for a place in the covered galleries, sixpence for the prominent "lord's rooms" to the side of the stage. In the indoor "private" theaters, gallants from the audience who fancied making themselves part of the spectacle sat on stools on the edge of the stage itself. Scholars debate as to how widespread this practice was in the public theaters such as the Globe. Once the audience were in place and the money counted, the gatherers were available to be extras on stage. That is one reason why battles and crowd scenes often come later rather than early in Shakespeare's plays. There was no formal prohibition upon performance by women, and there certainly were women among the gatherers, so it is not beyond the bounds of possibility that female crowd members were played by females.

The play began at two o'clock in the afternoon and the theater had to be cleared by five. After the main show, there would be a jig— which consisted not only of dancing, but also of knockabout comedy (it is the origin of the farcical "afterpiece" in the eighteenth-century theater). So the time available for a Shakespeare play was about two and a half hours, somewhere between the "two hours' traffic" mentioned in the prologue to *Romeo and Juliet* and the "three hours' spectacle" referred to in the preface to the 1647 Folio of Beaumont and Fletcher's plays. The prologue to a play by Thomas Middleton refers to a thousand lines as "one hour's words," so the likelihood is that about two and a half thousand, or a maximum of three thousand, lines made up the performed text. This is indeed the length of most of Shakespeare's comedies, whereas many of his tragedies and histories are much longer, raising the possibility that he wrote full scripts, possibly with eventual publication in mind, in the full knowledge that the stage version would be heavily cut. The short Quarto texts published in his lifetime—they used to be called "Bad" Quartos—provide fascinating evidence as to the kind of cutting that probably took place. So, for instance, the First Quarto of *Hamlet* neatly merges two occasions when Hamlet is overheard, the "Fishmonger" and the "nunnery" scenes.

The social composition of the audience was mixed. The poet Sir John Davies wrote of "A thousand townsmen, gentlemen and whores, / Porters and servingmen" who would "together throng" at the public playhouses. Though moralists associated female playgoing with adultery and the sex trade, many perfectly respectable citizens' wives were regular attendees. Some, no doubt, resembled the modern groupie: a story attested in two different sources has one citizen's wife making a post-show assignation with Richard Burbage and ending up in bed with Shakespeare—supposedly eliciting from the latter the quip that William the Conqueror was before Richard III. Defenders of theater liked to say that by witnessing the comeuppance of villains on the stage, audience members would repent of their own wrongdoings, but the reality is that most people went to the theater then, as they do now, for entertainment more than moral edification. Besides, it would be foolish to suppose that audiences behaved in a homogeneous way: a pamphlet of the 1630s tells of how two men went to see *Pericles* and one of them laughed while the other wept. Bishop John Hall complained that people went to church for the same reasons that they went to the theater: "for company, for custom, for recreation . . . to feed his eyes or his ears . . . or perhaps for sleep."

Men-about-town and clever young lawyers went to be seen as much as to see. In the modern popular imagination, shaped not least by *Shakespeare in Love* and the opening sequence of Laurence Olivier's *Henry V* film, the penny-paying groundlings stand in the yard hurling abuse or encouragement and hazelnuts or orange peel

at the actors, while the sophisticates in the covered galleries appreci-
ate Shakespeare's soaring poetry. The reality was probably the other
way around. A "groundling" was a kind of fish, so the nickname
suggests the penny audience standing below the level of the stage
and gazing in silent open-mouthed wonder at the spectacle unfold-
ing above them. The more difficult audience members, who kept up
a running commentary of clever remarks on the performance and
who occasionally got into quarrels with players, were the gallants.
Like Hollywood movies in modern times, Elizabethan and Jacobean
plays exercised a powerful influence on the fashion and behavior of
the young. John Marston mocks the lawyers who would open their
lips, perhaps to court a girl, and out would "flow / Naught but pure
Juliet and Romeo."

THE ENSEMBLE AT WORK

In the absence of typewriters and photocopying machines, reading
aloud would have been the means by which the company got to
know a new play. The tradition of the playwright reading his complete script to the assembled company endured for generations. A
copy would then have been taken to the Master of the Revels for
licensing. The theater book-holder or prompter would then have
copied the parts for distribution to the actors. A partbook consisted
of the character's lines, with each speech preceded by the last three
or four words of the speech before, the so-called "cue." These would
have been taken away and studied or "conned." During this period of
learning the parts, an actor might have had some one-to-one
instruction, perhaps from the dramatist, perhaps from a senior actor
who had played the same part before, and, in the case of an apprentice, from his master. A high percentage of Desdemona's lines occur
in dialogue with Othello, of Lady Macbeth's with Macbeth, Cleopatra's with Antony, and Volumnia's with Coriolanus. The roles would
almost certainly have been taken by the apprentice of the lead actor,
usually Burbage, who delivers the majority of the cues. Given that
apprentices lodged with their masters, there would have been ample
opportunity for personal instruction, which may be what made it
possible for young men to play such demanding parts.

9. Hypothetical reconstruction of the interior of an Elizabethan playhouse during a performance.

After the parts were learned, there may have been no more than a single rehearsal before the first performance. With six different plays to be put on every week, there was no time for more. Actors, then, would go into a show with a very limited sense of the whole. The notion of a collective rehearsal process that is itself a process of discovery for the actors is wholly modern and would have been incomprehensible to Shakespeare and his original ensemble. Given the number of parts an actor had to hold in his memory, the forgetting of lines was probably more frequent than in the modern theater. The book-holder was on hand to prompt.

Backstage personnel included the property man, the tire-man who oversaw the costumes, call boys, attendants, and the musicians, who might play at various times from the main stage, the rooms above, and within the tiring-house. Scriptwriters sometimes made a nuisance of themselves backstage. There was often tension between the acting companies and the freelance playwrights from whom they purchased scripts: it was a smart move on the part of Shakespeare and the Lord Chamberlain's Men to bring the writing process in-house.

Scenery was limited, though sometimes set pieces were brought on (a bank of flowers, a bed, the mouth of hell). The trapdoor from below, the gallery stage above, and the curtained discovery-space at the back allowed for an array of special effects: the rising of ghosts and apparitions, the descent of gods, dialogue between a character at a window and another at ground level, the revelation of a statue, or a pair of lovers playing at chess. Ingenious use could be made of props, as with the ass's head in *A Midsummer Night's Dream*. In a theater that does not clutter the stage with the material parapher-nalia of everyday life, those objects that are deployed may take on powerful symbolic weight, as when Shylock bears his weighing scales in one hand and knife in the other, thus becoming a parody of the figure of Justice, who traditionally bears a sword and a balance. Among the more significant items in the property cupboard of Shakespeare's company, there would have been a throne (the "chair of state"), joint stools, books, bottles, coins, purses, letters (which are brought on stage, read or referred to on about eighty occasions in the complete works), maps, gloves, a set of stocks (in which Kent is put in *King Lear*), rings, rapiers, daggers, broadswords, staves, pis-tols, masks and vizards, heads and skulls, torches and tapers and lanterns, which served to signal night scenes on the daylit stage, a buck's head, an ass's head, animal costumes. Live animals also put in appearances, most notably the dog Crab in *The Two Gentlemen of Verona* and possibly a young polar bear in *The Winter's Tale*.

The costumes were the most important visual dimension of the play. Playwrights were paid between £2 and £6 per script, whereas Alleyn was not averse to paying £20 for "a black velvet cloak with sleeves embroidered all with silver and gold." No matter the period of the play, actors always wore contemporary costume. The excitement for the audience came not from any impression of historical accuracy, but from the richness of the attire and perhaps the transgressive thrill of the knowledge that here were commoners like themselves strutting in the costumes of courtiers in effective defiance of the strict sumptu-ary laws whereby in real life people had to wear the clothes that befit-ted their social station.

To an even greater degree than props, costumes could carry symbolic importance. Racial characteristics could be suggested: a breastplate and helmet for a Roman soldier, a turban for a Turk, long robes for exotic characters such as Moors, a gabardine for a Jew. The figure of Time, as in *The Winter's Tale*, would be equipped with hourglass, scythe, and wings; Rumour, who speaks the prologue of *2 Henry IV*, wore a costume adorned with a thousand tongues. The wardrobe in the tiring-house of the Globe would have contained much of the same stock as that of rival manager Philip Henslowe at the Rose: green gowns for outlaws and foresters, black for melancholy men such as Jaques and people in mourning such as the Countess in *All's Well That Ends Well* (at the beginning of *Hamlet*, the prince is still in mourning black when everyone else is in festive garb for the wedding of the new king), a gown and hood for a friar (or a feigned friar like the duke in *Measure for Measure*), blue coats and tawny to distinguish the followers of rival factions, a leather apron and ruler for a carpenter (as in the opening scene of *Julius Caesar*—and in *A Midsummer Night's Dream*, where this is the only sign that Peter Quince is a carpenter), a cockle hat with staff and a pair of sandals for a pilgrim or palmer (the disguise assumed by Helen in *All's Well*), bodices and kirtles with farthingales beneath for the boys who are to be dressed as girls. A gender switch such as that of Rosalind or Jessica seems to have taken between fifty and eighty lines of dialogue—Viola does not resume her "maiden weeds," but remains in her boy's costume to the end of *Twelfth Night* because a change would have slowed down the action at just the moment it was speeding to a climax. Henslowe's inventory also included "a robe for to go invisible": Oberon, Puck, and Ariel must have had something similar.

As the costumes appealed to the eyes, so there was music for the ears. Comedies included many songs. Desdemona's willow song, perhaps a late addition to the text, is a rare and thus exceptionally poignant example from tragedy. Trumpets and tuckets sounded for ceremonial entrances, drums denoted an army on the march. Background music could create atmosphere, as at the beginning of *Twelfth Night*, during the lovers' dialogue near the end of *The Merchant of Venice*, when the statue seemingly comes to life in *The Winter's Tale*, and for the revival of Pericles and of Lear (in the Quarto text, but not the Folio). The haunting sound of the hautboy suggested a realm beyond the human, as when the god Hercules is imagined deserting Mark Antony. Dances symbolized the harmony of the end of a comedy—though in Shakespeare's world of mingled joy and sorrow, someone is usually left out of the circle.

The most important resource was, of course, the actors themselves. They needed many skills: in the words of one contemporary commentator, "dancing, activity, music, song, elocution, ability of body, memory, skill of weapon, pregnancy of wit." Their bodies were as significant as their voices. Hamlet tells the player to "suit the action to the word, the word to the action": moments of strong emotion, known as "passions," relied on a repertoire of dramatic gestures as well as a modulation of the voice. When Titus Andronicus has had his hand chopped off, he asks "How can I grace my talk, / Wanting a hand to give it action?" A pen portrait of "The Character of an Excellent Actor" by the dramatist John Webster is almost certainly based on his impression of Shakespeare's leading man, Richard Burbage: "By a full and significant action of body, he charms our attention: sit in a full theater, and you will think you see so many lines drawn from the circumference of so many ears, whiles the actor is the centre. . . ."

Though Burbage was admired above all others, praise was also heaped upon the apprentice players whose alto voices fitted them for the parts of women. A spectator at Oxford in 1610 records how the audience were reduced to tears by the pathos of Desdemona's death. The puritans who fumed about the biblical prohibition upon crossdressing and the encouragement to sodomy constituted by the sight of an adult male kissing a teenage boy onstage were a small minority. Little is known, however, about the characteristics of the leading apprentices in Shakespeare's company. It may perhaps be inferred that one was a lot taller than the other, since Shakespeare often wrote for a pair of female friends, one tall and fair, the other short and dark (Helena and Hermia, Rosalind and Celia, Beatrice and Hero).

We know little about Shakespeare's own acting roles—an early allusion indicates that he often took royal parts, and a venerable tradition gives him old Adam in *As You Like It* and the ghost of old King Hamlet. Save for Burbage's lead roles and the generic part of the clown, all such castings are mere speculation. We do not even know for sure whether the original Falstaff was Will Kempe or another actor who specialized in comic roles, Thomas Pope.

Kempe left the company in early 1599. Tradition has it that he fell out with Shakespeare over the matter of excessive improvisation. He was replaced by Robert Armin, who was less of a clown and more of a cerebral wit: this explains the difference between such parts as Lancelet Gobbo and Dogberry, which were written for Kempe, and the more verbally sophisticated Feste and Lear's Fool, which were written for Armin.

One thing that is clear from surviving "plots" or storyboards of plays from the period is that a degree of doubling was necessary. *2 Henry VI* has over sixty speaking parts, but more than half of the characters only appear in a single scene and most scenes have only six to eight speakers. At a stretch, the play could be performed by thirteen actors. When Thomas Platter saw *Julius Caesar* at the Globe in 1599, he noted that there were about fifteen. Why doesn't Paris go to the Capulet ball in *Romeo and Juliet?* Perhaps because he was doubled with Mercutio, who does. In *The Winter's Tale*, Mamillius might have come back as Perdita and Antigonus been doubled by Camillo, making the partnership with Paulina at the end a very neat touch. Titania and Oberon are often played by the same pair as Hippolyta and Theseus, suggesting a symbolic matching of the rulers of the worlds of night and day, but it is questionable whether there would have been time for the necessary costume changes. As so often, one is left in a realm of tantalizing speculation.

THE KING'S MAN

On Queen Elizabeth's death in 1603, the new king, James I, who had held the Scottish throne as James VI since he had been an infant, immediately took the Lord Chamberlain's Men under his direct patronage. Henceforth they would be the King's Men, and for the rest of Shakespeare's career they were favored with far more court performances than any of their rivals. There even seem to have been rumors early in the reign that Shakespeare and Burbage were being considered for knighthoods, an unprecedented honor for mere actors—and one that in the event was not accorded to a member of the profession for nearly three hundred years, when the title was bestowed upon Henry Irving, the leading Shakespearean actor of Queen Victoria's reign.

Shakespeare's productivity rate slowed in the Jacobean years, not because of age or some personal trauma, but because there were frequent outbreaks of plague, causing the theaters to be closed for long periods. The King's Men were forced to spend many months on the road. Between November 1603 and 1608, they were to be found at various towns in the south and Midlands, though Shakespeare probably did not tour with them by this time. He had bought a large house back home in Stratford and was accumulating other property. He may indeed have stopped acting soon after the new king took the throne. With the London theaters closed so much of the time and a large repertoire on the stocks, Shakespeare seems to have focused his energies on writing a few long and complex tragedies that could have been played on demand at court: *Othello*, *King Lear*, *Antony and Cleopatra*, *Coriolanus*, and *Cymbeline* are among his longest and poetically grandest plays. *Macbeth* only survives in a shorter text, which shows signs of adaptation after Shakespeare's death. The bitterly satirical *Timon of Athens*, apparently a collaboration with Thomas Middleton that may have failed on the stage, also belongs to this period. In comedy, too, he wrote longer and morally darker works than in the Elizabethan period, pushing at the very bounds of the form in *Measure for Measure* and *All's Well That Ends Well*.

From 1608 onward, when the King's Men began occupying the indoor Blackfriars playhouse (as a winter house, meaning that they only used the outdoor Globe in summer?), Shakespeare turned to a more romantic style. His company had a great success with a revived and altered version of an old pastoral play called *Mucedorus*. It even featured a bear. The younger dramatist John Fletcher, meanwhile, sometimes working in collaboration with Francis Beaumont, was pioneering a new style of tragicomedy, a mix of romance and royalism laced with intrigue and pastoral excursions. Shakespeare experimented with this idiom in *Cymbeline* and it was presumably with his blessing that Fletcher eventually took over as the King's Men's company dramatist. The two writers apparently collaborated on three plays in the years 1612–14: a lost romance called *Cardenio* (based on the love-madness of a character in Cervantes' *Don Quixote*), *Henry VIII* (originally staged with the title "All Is True"), and *The Two Noble Kinsmen*, a dramatization of Chaucer's "Knight's Tale." These were written after Shakespeare's two final solo-authored plays, *The Winter's Tale*, a self-consciously old-fashioned work dramatizing the pastoral romance of his old enemy Robert Greene, and *The Tempest*, which at one and the same time drew together multiple theatrical traditions, diverse reading, and contemporary interest in the fate of a ship that had been wrecked on the way to the New World.

The collaborations with Fletcher suggest that Shakespeare's career ended with a slow fade rather than the sudden retirement supposed by the nineteenth-century Romantic critics who read Prospero's epilogue to *The Tempest* as Shakespeare's personal farewell to his art. In the last few years of his life Shakespeare certainly spent more of his time in Stratford-upon-Avon, where he became further involved in property dealing and litigation. But his London life also continued. In 1613 he made his first major London property purchase: a freehold house in the Blackfriars district, close to his company's indoor theater. *The Two Noble Kinsmen* may have been written as late as 1614, and Shakespeare was in London on business a little over a year before he died of an unknown cause at home in Stratford-upon-Avon in 1616, probably on his fifty-second birthday.

About half the sum of his works were published in his lifetime, in texts of variable quality. A few years after his death, his fellow actors began putting together an authorized edition of his complete *Comedies, Histories and Tragedies*. It appeared in 1623, in large "Folio" format. This collection of thirty-six plays gave Shakespeare his immortality. In the words of his fellow dramatist Ben Jonson, who contributed two poems of praise at the start of the Folio, the body of his work made him "a monument without a tomb":

And art alive still while thy book doth live
And we have wits to read and praise to give . . .
He was not of an age, but for all time!

SHAKESPEARE'S WORKS: A CHRONOLOGY

1589–91	*? Arden of Faversham* (possible part authorship)
1589–92	*The Taming of the Shrew*
1589–92	*? Edward the Third* (possible part authorship)
1591	*The Second Part of Henry the Sixth*, originally called *The First Part of the Contention betwixt the Two Famous Houses of York and Lancaster* (element of coauthorship possible)
1591	*The Third Part of Henry the Sixth*, originally called *The True Tragedy of Richard Duke of York* (element of coauthorship probable)
1591–92	*The Two Gentlemen of Verona*
1591–92; perhaps revised 1594	*The Lamentable Tragedy of Titus Andronicus* (probably cowritten with, or revising an earlier version by, George Peele)
1592	*The First Part of Henry the Sixth*, probably with Thomas Nashe and others
1592/94	*King Richard the Third*
1593	*Venus and Adonis* (poem)
1593–94	*The Rape of Lucrece* (poem)
1593–1608	*Sonnets* (154 poems, published 1609 with *A Lover's Complaint*, a poem of disputed authorship)
1592–94/ 1600–03	*Sir Thomas More* (a single scene for a play originally by Anthony Munday, with other revisions by Henry Chettle, Thomas Dekker, and Thomas Heywood)
1594	*The Comedy of Errors*
1595	*Love's Labour's Lost*

1595–97	*Love's Labour's Won* (a lost play, unless the original title for another comedy)
1595–96	*A Midsummer Night's Dream*
1595–96	*The Tragedy of Romeo and Juliet*
1595–96	*King Richard the Second*
1595–97	*The Life and Death of King John* (possibly earlier)
1596–97	*The Merchant of Venice*
1596–97	*The First Part of Henry the Fourth*
1597–98	*The Second Part of Henry the Fourth*
1598	*Much Ado About Nothing*
1598–99	*The Passionate Pilgrim* (20 poems, some not by Shakespeare)
1599	*The Life of Henry the Fifth*
1599	"To the Queen" (epilogue for a court performance)
1599	*As You Like It*
1599	*The Tragedy of Julius Caesar*
1600–01	*The Tragedy of Hamlet, Prince of Denmark* (perhaps revising an earlier version)
1600–01	*The Merry Wives of Windsor* (perhaps revising version of 1597–99)
1601	"Let the Bird of Loudest Lay" (poem, known since 1807 as "The Phoenix and Turtle" [turtle-dove])
1601	*Twelfth Night, or What You Will*
1601–02	*The Tragedy of Troilus and Cressida*
1604	*The Tragedy of Othello, the Moor of Venice*
1604	*Measure for Measure*
1605	*All's Well That Ends Well*
1605	*The Life of Timon of Athens*, with Thomas Middleton
1605–06	*The Tragedy of King Lear*
1605–08	? contribution to *The Four Plays in One* (lost, except for *A Yorkshire Tragedy*, mostly by Thomas Middleton)

1606	*The Tragedy of Macbeth* (surviving text has additional scenes by Thomas Middleton)
1606–07	*The Tragedy of Antony and Cleopatra*
1608	*The Tragedy of Coriolanus*
1608	*Pericles, Prince of Tyre*, with George Wilkins
1610	*The Tragedy of Cymbeline*
1611	*The Winter's Tale*
1611	*The Tempest*
1612–13	*Cardenio*, with John Fletcher (survives only in later adaptation called *Double Falsehood* by Lewis Theobald)
1613	*Henry VIII (All Is True)*, with John Fletcher
1613–14	*The Two Noble Kinsmen*, with John Fletcher

FURTHER READING
AND VIEWING

CRITICAL APPROACHES

Atkin, Graham, *Twelfth Night: Character Studies* (2008). Detailed account of the characters.

Barber, C. L., *Shakespeare's Festive Comedies* (1959). One of the best critical books on Shakespeare ever written.

Berry, Ralph, *Changing Styles in Shakespeare* (1981). Chapter 6, "The Season of *Twelfth Night*," pp. 109–19, argues that 1950 was the point when sensibilities changed and it became a less comic, more serious play.

Ford, John R., *Twelfth Night: A Guide to the Play* (2006). Useful chapters on textual history, sources, structure, themes, critical approaches and performance.

Frye, Northrop, *A Natural Perspective: The Development of Shakespearean Comedy and Romance* (1965). A slim work of supreme power.

Hotson, Leslie, *The First Night of Twelfth Night* (1954). Fascinating account, with ingenious detective work and lots of historical details, though the case for the occasion of the first night is not finally proven.

Maslen, R. W., *Shakespeare and Comedy* (2005). Sets the Elizabethan comedies in the context of both theatrical traditions and anti-stage polemic.

Massai, Sonia, ed., *William Shakespeare's Twelfth Night: A Sourcebook* (2007). Thorough account of social context, critical history, and performance.

Palmer, D. J., ed., *Shakespeare: Twelfth Night: A Casebook* (1972). Broad collection of early criticism and influential twentieth-century studies.

Potter, Lois, *Twelfth Night: Text and Performance* (1985). Part 1, a useful introduction to the text; Part 2 focuses on productions from 1969 to 1982.

Smith, Bruce R., *William Shakespeare: Twelfth Night: Texts and Contexts* (2001). Detailed account of socio-cultural context.

White, R. S., ed., *Twelfth Night: New Casebooks* (1996). Theoretically informed selection of essays.

THE PLAY IN PERFORMANCE

Billington, Michael, *Approaches to Twelfth Night*, Directors' Shakespeare (1990). Illuminating accounts by a variety of modern directors.

Brockbank, Philip, ed., *Players of Shakespeare* (1985). Actors' firsthand accounts: chapter 4, Donald Sinden on playing Malvolio, pp. 41–66.

Edmondson, Paul, *Twelfth Night*, Shakespeare Handbooks (2005). Detailed commentary, very good on performance.

Fielding, Emma, *Twelfth Night*, Actors on Shakespeare (2002). Thoughtful, engaging account of playing Viola with the RSC.

Jackson, Russell, and Robert Smallwood, eds., *Players of Shakespeare 2* (1988). Zoë Wanamaker as Viola in *Twelfth Night*, pp. 81–92.

Nunn, Trevor, *William Shakespeare's Twelfth Night* (1996). Screenplay of film plus introduction.

Parsons, Keith, and Pamela Mason, *Shakespeare in Performance* (1995). Useful introduction by Elizabeth Schafer, lavish illustrations, pp. 227–32.

Pennington, Michael, *Twelfth Night: A User's Guide* (2000). Detailed account, arising from English Shakespeare Company's 1991 production, unpretentious and readable.

Smallwood, Robert, ed., *Players of Shakespeare 5* (2003). Zoë Waites and Matilda Ziegler on playing Viola and Olivia, pp. 60–73.

AVAILABLE ON DVD

Twelfth Night, directed by John Sichel (1969, DVD 2009). Originally produced for television, with Ralph Richardson as Sir Toby, Alec Guinness as Malvolio, and Tommy Steele as a youthful Feste, with Joan Plowright playing both Viola and Sebastian.

Twelfth Night, The Animated Tales directed by Maria Muat (1995, DVD 2007). Excellent Welsh-Russian collaboration with screenplay adapted by Leon Garfield, voiced by Alec McCowan, Michael Kitchen, and Suzanne Burden.

Twelfth Night, directed by John Gorrie for BBC Shakespeare (1980, DVD 2005). One of the best in this series, starring Alec McCowan, Robert Hardy, Robert Lindsay, and Felicity Kendall as Viola.

Twelfth Night, directed by Kenneth Branagh (1988, DVD 2004). Based on Renaissance Theatre Company's stage version, starring Richard Briers, Frances Barber, and Anton Lesser.

Twelfth Night, directed by Tim Supple (1988, DVD 2005). Starring Parminder Nagra and Chiwetel Ejiofor in a contemporary update, set in multi-cultural London.

Twelfth Night, directed by Trevor Nunn (1996, DVD 2001). Star-studded cast in a highly intelligent and nuanced reading, including Imogen Stubbs, Toby Stephens, and Helena Bonham-Carter.

She's the Man, directed by Andy Fickman (2006). Updated American high-school rom-com starring Amanda Bynes as Viola and Channing Tatum as Duke Orsino.

REFERENCES

1. John Manningham, *The Diary of John Manningham of the Middle Temple, 1602–1603* (1976), p. 48.
2. Leslie Hotson, *The First Night of Twelfth Night* (1954).
3. Leonard Digges' prefatory poem to William Shakespeare, *Poems* (1640), reprinted in 1979 with introduction and notes by Holger M. Klein.
4. Samuel Pepys, *The Diary of Samuel Pepys*, 20 January 1669, ed. Robert Latham and William Matthews, Vol. 9, 1668–69 (1976).
5. John R. Ford, *Twelfth Night: A Guide to the Play* (2006), p. 137.
6. Ford, *Twelfth Night*, p. 139.
7. Charles Lamb, "On Some of the Old Actors," from *Essays of Elia* (1835), p. 149.
8. William Archer, "*Twelfth Night* at the Lyceum," *Macmillan's Magazine*, Vol. L, August 1884, pp. 271–9.
9. Archer, "*Twelfth Night* at the Lyceum."
10. William Archer, review of *Twelfth Night* in *The Theatrical "World" of 1894* (1895), pp. 22–31.
11. George Bernard Shaw quoted in *Shakespearean Criticism*, Vol. 26, ed. Michael Magoulias (1995), p. 196.
12. George Odell, *Shakespeare from Betterton to Irving*, Vol. 2 (1921), p. 455.
13. Ford, *Twelfth Night*, p. 143, quoting Elizabeth Story Donno's *New Cambridge Shakespeare* (2004), p. 31.
14. Michael Billington, "*Twelfth Night*: A Stage History," in *Directors' Shakespeare: Approaches to "Twelfth Night"* by Bill Alexander and others, ed. Michael Billington (1990), pp. ix–xxxi.
15. Billington, "*Twelfth Night*: A Stage History."
16. Harley Granville-Barker, *Prefaces to Shakespeare*, Vol. 6, p. 30.
17. Billington, "*Twelfth Night*: A Stage History."
18. Grenville Vernon, *The Commonweal*, Vol. 7, 6 December 1940.
19. T. C. Worsley, *New Statesman and Nation*, Vol. XL, No. 1029, 25 November 1950, pp. 498–500.
20. J. C. Trewin, *Illustrated London News*, Vol. 217, No. 5825, 9 December 1950, p. 962.
21. John Gielgud, *An Actor and His Time* (1979), p. 176.
22. Peter Fleming, *Spectator*, Vol. 194, No. 6617, 22 April 1955, p. 502.

23. Billington, "*Twelfth Night*: A Stage History."

24. Henry Hewes, *Saturday Review*, New York, Vol. XL, No. 29, 20 July 1957, p. 26.

25. Arnold Edinborough, "Canada's Permanent Elizabethan Theatre," *Shakespeare Quarterly*, Vol. VIII, No. 4, Autumn 1957, pp. 511–14.

26. John Wain, *Observer*, 27 April 1958.

27. Alan Brien, *Spectator*, Vol. 200, No. 6775, 2 May 1958.

28. Peter Jackson, *Plays and Players*, Vol. 5, No. 9, June 1958, p. 13.

29. Robert Speaight, *Shakespeare Quarterly*, Vol. XI, No. 4, Autumn 1960, pp. 449–51.

30. *Shakespearean Criticism*, Vol. 26, p. 199.

31. Billington, "*Twelfth Night*: A Stage History."

32. Billington, "*Twelfth Night*: A Stage History."

33. Ford, *Twelfth Night*, p. 155.

34. Ford, *Twelfth Night*, p. 155.

35. Ford, *Twelfth Night*, p. 157.

36. Billington, "*Twelfth Night*: A Stage History."

37. Kenneth S. Rothwell, *A History of Shakespeare on Screen: A Century of Film and Television* (1999), p. 11.

38. Ford, *Twelfth Night*, p. 160.

39. Ford, *Twelfth Night*, p. 163.

40. Ford, *Twelfth Night*, p. 161.

41. Ford, *Twelfth Night*, p. 161.

42. Ford, *Twelfth Night*, p. 161.

43. Percy Bysshe Shelley, *A Defence of Poetry* (1821).

44. Ralph Berry, *Changing Styles in Shakespeare* (1981).

45. Irving Wardle, London *Times*, 7 August 1970.

46. Hilary Spurling, *Spectator*, 30 August 1969.

47. Anne Barton, *Twelfth Night* RSC program note, 1969.

48. Berry, *Changing Styles in Shakespeare*.

49. Lois Potter, *Twelfth Night: Text and Performance* (1985).

50. Sheila Bannock, *Stratford-upon-Avon Herald*, 29 August 1969.

51. Robert Speaight, *Shakespeare Quarterly*, Vol. 20, 1969.

52. Jeremy Kingston, *Punch*, 3 September 1969.

53. Wardle, *The Times*, 7 August 1970.

54. Michael Magoulias, ed., *Shakespearean Criticism*, Vol. 26 (1995).

55. James Fenton, London *Sunday Times*, 24 April 1983.

56. Magoulias, *Shakespearean Criticism*.

57. Nicholas de Jongh, *Evening Standard*, 26 May 1994.

58. Ian Judge, *Twelfth Night* RSC program note, 1994.

59. James Treadwell, *Spectator*, 6 December 1997.

60. Carole Woddis, *What's On*, 3 December 1997.

61. Janice Wardle, "*Twelfth Night*: 'One Face, One Voice, One Habit, and Two Persons!,' " in *Talking Shakespeare*, ed. Deborah Cartmell and Michael Scott (2001).

62. Michael Billington, *Guardian*, 27 November 1997.

63. Charles Spencer, *Daily Telegraph*, 27 November 1997.

64. Judi Dench quoted by Wardle, "Twelfth Night."

65. Berry, *Changing Styles in Shakespeare*.

66. Bill Alexander, "A Director's View—A Personal Essay," in *Twelfth Night*, ed. Neil King, Longman Study Texts (1989).

67. Joseph H. Summers, RSC *Twelfth Night* program, 1969.

68. Alexander in King, *Twelfth Night*.

69. Elizabeth Schafer, "Twelfth Night," in Parson and Mason (eds.), *Shakespeare in Performance*, 1995.

70. François Laroque, *Cahiers Élisabethains*, No. 32, October 1987.

71. Alexander, "A Director's View."

72. Patrick Carnegy, *Spectator*, 14 May 2005.

73. Donald Sinden quoted in " 'There is no slander in an allowed fool': Comics, Clowns and Fools," in Judith Cook, *Shakespeare's Players* (1983).

74. Lisa Jardine, *Twelfth Night* RSC program note, 1994.

75. Jan Kott, *Twelfth Night* RSC program note, 1994.

76. Magoulias, *Shakespearean Criticism*.

77. Irving Wardle, London *Times*, 23 August 1974.

78. Michael Billington, *Guardian*, 23 August 1974.

79. Bernard Crick, *Times Higher Educational Supplement*, 14 March 1975.

80. Jane Lapotaire quoted in Judith Cook, *Women in Shakespeare* (1980).

81. Potter, *Twelfth Night*.

82. Nicholas de Jongh, *Evening Standard*, 11 May 2001.

83. Patrick Carnegy, *Spectator*, 19 May 2001.

84. Zoë Waites and Matilda Ziegler, "Viola and Olivia in Twelfth Night," in *Players of Shakespeare 5*, ed. Robert Smallwood (2003).

85. John Caird, interview with Michael Billington, *Director's Shakespeare: Approaches to Twelfth Night* (1990).

86. Terry Hands, interview with Billington, *Approaches to Twelfth Night*.

87. Michael Coveney, *Financial Times*, 6 February 1975.

88. John Caird, interview with Billington, *Approaches to Twelfth Night*.

89. Jan Kott, *Shakespeare Our Contemporary* (1964).

90. Potter, *Twelfth Night*.

91. Elizabeth Schafer, "Twelfth Night," in *Shakespeare in Performance*, ed. Keith Parsons and Pamela Mason (1995).

92. Carnegy, *Spectator*, 14 May 2005.

93. Nigel Hess, *Twelfth Night* RSC program note, 1994.

94. Peter Thomson, *Shakespeare Survey*, Vol. 28, 1975.

95. Thomson, *Shakespeare Survey*.

96. Barton, *Twelfth Night* RSC program note.

97. Wardle, "*Twelfth Night*."

98. W. E. Burghardt Du Bois, *The Souls of Black Folk: Essays and Sketches* (1903), chapter 7.

ACKNOWLEDGMENTS AND PICTURE CREDITS

Preparation of "*Twelfth Night* in Performance" was assisted by a generous grant from the CAPITAL Centre (Creativity and Performance in Teaching and Learning) of the University of Warwick for research in the RSC archive at the Shakespeare Birthplace Trust. The Arts and Humanities Research Council (AHRC) funded a term's research leave that enabled Jonathan Bate to work on "The Director's Cut."

Picture research by Michelle Morton. Grateful acknowledgment is made to the Shakespeare Birthplace Trust for assistance with picture research (special thanks to Helen Hargest) and reproduction fees.

Images of RSC productions are supplied by the Shakespeare Centre Library and Archive, Stratford-upon-Avon. This Library, maintained by the Shakespeare Birthplace Trust, holds the most important collection of Shakespeare material in the UK, including the Royal Shakespeare Company's official archive. It is open to the public free of charge.

For more information see www.shakespeare.org.uk.

1. London Savoy Theatre, directed by Harley Granville-Barker (1912). Reproduced by permission of the Shakespeare Birthplace Trust
2. Directed by Bill Alexander (1987). Joe Cocks Studio Collection © Shakespeare Birthplace Trust
3. Directed by Peter Gill (1974). Joe Cocks Studio Collection © Shakespeare Birthplace Trust
4. Directed by Lindsay Posner (2001). Manuel Harlan © Royal Shakespeare Company
5. Directed by Michael Boyd (2005). Ellie Kurttz © Royal Shakespeare Company
6. Directed by Declan Donnellan (2006). Ellie Kurttz © Royal Shakespeare Company

7. Directed by Sam Mendes (2002) © Donald Cooper/photostage .co.uk

8. Directed by Neil Bartlett (2007). Hugo Glendinning © Royal Shakespeare Company

9. Reconstructed Elizabethan Playhouse © Charcoalblue

MODERN LIBRARY IS ONLINE AT WWW.MODERNLIBRARY.COM

MODERN LIBRARY ONLINE IS YOUR GUIDE
TO CLASSIC LITERATURE ON THE WEB

THE MODERN LIBRARY E-NEWSLETTER

Our free e-mail newsletter is sent to subscribers, and features sample chapters, interviews with and essays by our authors, upcoming books, special promotions, announcements, and news. To subscribe to the Modern Library e-newsletter, visit **www.modernlibrary.com**

THE MODERN LIBRARY WEBSITE

Check out the Modern Library website at
www.modernlibrary.com for:

- The Modern Library e-newsletter
- A list of our current and upcoming titles and series
- Reading Group Guides and exclusive author spotlights
- Special features with information on the classics and other paperback series
- Excerpts from new releases and other titles
- A list of our e-books and information on where to buy them
- The Modern Library Editorial Board's 100 Best Novels and 100 Best Nonfiction Books of the Twentieth Century written in the English language
- News and announcements

Questions? E-mail us at **modernlibrary@randomhouse.com**.
For questions about examination or desk copies, please visit
the Random House Academic Resources site at
www.randomhouse.com/academic